P9-BZU-800

Myra Brown
1523 W. Sadler Hill Rd.
Logansport, IN 46947-6804

THE RIVER NILE

THE RIVER

NILE

BY BRUCE BRANDER
National Geographic Staff

FOREWORD BY MELVILLE BELL GROSVENOR
President and Editor, National Geographic Society

PREPARED BY NATIONAL GEOGRAPHIC
SPECIAL PUBLICATIONS DIVISION
Robert L. Breeden, Chief

NATIONAL GEOGRAPHIC SOCIETY
WASHINGTON, D.C.

OVERLEAF: CARGO-LADEN NAGGARS, CALLED FELUCCAS ALONG THE NILE, GLIDE THROUGH THE DELTA; HELEN AND FRANK SCHREIDER, N.G.S. STAFF; RENE BURRI (ABOVE)

Poised in mystery, figures and hieroglyphs from a tomb at Saqqâra evoke the splendor of ancient Egypt.

THE RIVER NILE by Bruce Brander, Special Publications Staff; Gilbert M. Grosvenor, Editorial Director

The second in a series of National Geographic books from the Special Publications Division, produced by the following st

Robert L. Breeden, *Editor*
Donald J. Crump, *Assistant Editor*
Robert L. Conly, *Manuscript Editor*
Mary Ann Harrell, *Assistant to the Editor*
David R. Bridge, *Picture Editor*
Joseph A. Taney, *Art Director*
Josephine B. Bolt, *Assistant Art Director*
Johanna G. Farren, *Research*
Ronald M. Fisher, *Production;* Luba Balko, *Assistant*
Editorial Staff: Richard M. Crum, Tadd Fisher, Louise Graves,
Carolyn Hatt, Geraldine Linder, Frank Sartwell, Peggy Winston;
Margaret S. Dean, Rose Marie English, *Assistants*
James R. Whitney and William W. Smith, *Engraving and Printing*
Dorothy Corson, *Index*

 Library of Congress Catalog Card No. 66-18848

Front Endsheet: The mighty Nile etches the face of the African continent. *Painting by Ken Fagg*

FOREWORD

OUR JET FLEW SMOOTHLY through the night, yet I was too excited to sleep. Moonlight etched the horizon for a hundred-mile view, vast as the ocean, of undulating Sahara dunes. Slithering like a snake, the great river came into focus. Then the moon caught it: For one jet-borne instant the water dazzled bright, flashing my own first glimpse of the River Nile.

The jet was taking me from Rome to Khartoum in little more than six hours. Instead of shrinking distance, the plane meted out the truly enormous scope of time and space: from the golden city of the Caesars to the grit of Kitchener's last cavalry charge. The Nile unites all eras. Throughout the night, my thoughts roamed back to articles that had crossed my desk in years gone by.

"The noonday sun was hot . . ." wrote Maynard Owen Williams in the NATIONAL GEOGRAPHIC of May, 1923. "Thus should one approach that hell-hole in the hills where the greatest Pharaohs hid themselves. . . ." So read his eyewitness report as the wondrous tomb of Tutankhamun was officially opened.

Pharaohs, pyramids, Roman legions—they ornament the pageant of the Nile. Napoleon's soldiers enter and stumble on the Rosetta Stone. Rommel's tanks advance, then flee before Montgomery. And now engineers toy with generators the size of sphinxes at the Aswân High Dam.

Upstream, the river nourishes big game—and high adventure. "You chaps are committing triple suicide," one district commissioner told John M. Goddard and two companions when they undertook to navigate the Nile by kayak. The pessimist was nearly right. Before they were done, the men had burned with malarial fevers, dodged puff adders, and narrowly missed drowning uncounted times. Taking photographs ashore, Goddard met an elephant that "lashed the air with his trunk" and "charged me. I turned and ran, flinging my kayak into the river . . . before Jumbo thundered to the water's edge." Goddard lived to bring back his tales and pictures for NATIONAL GEOGRAPHIC.

Those photographs and thousands of others were part of the Society archives studied by staff writer Bruce Brander before he left on his two far-ranging Nile expeditions.

Home again, he presented me with a bottle of clear water, a souvenir from a small spring in the Burundi hills: the southernmost source of the Nile. It recalled an ancient Egyptian proverb: "He who once drinks the water of the Nile . . . will return to drink again." The knowledge and lore of the Nile are like its waters. And in this spirit, your Society offers this book to read and read again—a volume as compelling as the River Nile itself.

Melville Bell Grosvenor

NATIONAL GEOGRAPHIC PHOTOGRAPHER WINFIELD PARKS

As evening falls, women of Qena in Egypt fill earthenware jars with water drawn from the Nile.

CONTENTS

NATIONAL GEOGRAPHIC PHOTOGRAPHER WINFIELD PARKS

Prologue

1

SOUTH TO THE SOURCE

"SIX MONTHS AGO, you wouldn't have dared go back into these hills," Captain Paddy O'Reilly shouted over the roar of a single engine. The propeller tugged our plane over a damp green mountaintop, and Paddy aimed the nose down again. Angry clouds fumed like dry ice a few yards above the cockpit. The Irish pilot skimmed under them for visibility, flying so low that we could single out a tribesman in a white mantle hoeing his banana patch with the metal-bladed club farmers use in the Kingdom of Burundi.

"A prince was assassinated," Paddy explained, "and the king's army came back here taking reprisals. It wasn't wise to go wandering about just then." He smoothed a black goatee and lighted a fresh East Africa Sweet Menthol cigarette with the stub of an old one. "Things are calm now, though. You shouldn't have any trouble."

He meant only political trouble, which staff photographer Joseph Scherschel and I had not even considered. The roads worried us more. Somewhere below a red clay track twisted through the tumbled landscape of Burundi to our first goal along the Nile—the river's southernmost source. Now, the region's long rainy season might be turning it to a porridge of mud.

"Do you think we'll get a car through?" Joe shouted from the plane's rear seat. Pellets of rain burst on the Plexiglas around us, roaring almost as loud as the engine.

"I guess we could walk," I volunteered, though I wondered if even that was feasible. I knew very little of the conditions that we would meet here, and on many other

Landmark of civilization, the Great Pyramid at Gîza, raised 4,500 years ago, provides a resting place at sunset for a guide. With the Monument of Chephren (center) it defies time on the west bank of the Nile near Cairo.

GILBERT H. GROSVENOR (ABOVE) AND JOHN M. GODDAR

NATIONAL GEOGRAPHIC PHOTOGRAPHER WINFIELD PARKS

Geographic Adventurers Follow the Course of the Nile

For more than 60 years, writers and photographers have captured the saga of the Nile, its peoples, and its ancient splendors for the NATIONAL GEOGRAPHIC.

"Nowhere can you see more dramatically than along the Nile that water is life," wrote Elsie May Bell Grosvenor in 1954. She rides a camel at the Pyramids and Sphinx, accompanying her husband, Dr. Gilbert H. Grosvenor, Editor of the Magazine for 55 years (above, left).

". . . the Nile has influenced, somehow, every person living in our Western World today," reported John M. Goddard in 1955. By kayak he and his two companions (left) braved hazards of the world's longest river.

Almost a decade later the Nile bore the world-roving owners of the ketch *Yankee* past the imposing cliff-cut temples of Ramesses II (above) at Abu Simbel. Captain Irving Johnson and his wife Electa climb down from the colossi (right), today raised above the dammed-up Nile. "We would sail one of the most traveled waterways—and be among the last to see a storied section of it," wrote the Johnsons.

NATIONAL GEOGRAPHIC PHOTOGRAPHER WINFIELD PARKS

seldom-traveled stretches of the Nile. For thousands of years, men have written about this monarch of all rivers. But few accounts trace it from end to end. And those that do all tell a somewhat different story—about roads and shipping, about people and their ways of living. Certainly ours would too.

I had realized that at the very beginning of our journey. Planning to travel the first part of the Nile together, Joe and I met in Athens, then stopped at Cairo on our way south. In a single day there, we found a city greatly changed, and changing still. Steel skeletons scratched the sky, waiting for skins of concrete and aluminum. Suburbs sprawled outward, bringing people, shops, buses, and trees into the desert. Western music, clothing, and food mixed more strongly than ever with rhythms, turbans, and cooking smells of old Egypt.

WHEN OUR JET ROSE above Cairo and turned upstream, we found a more familiar Nile. People who read "Recent Discoveries in Egypt" in a 1901 issue of NATIONAL GEOGRAPHIC could recognize the land that slipped under us at ten miles a minute. Pyramids lump the riverbank, unchanging as the centuries pass. Bedouin still raise their tents among the desert dunes. And on the thin green rope of life along the Nile, farmers use tools like those pictured in ancient tombs.

Not until we came to southern Egypt did we see vast and sudden change. The river's green water was crawling outward behind the Aswân High Dam, making a lake on the desert. As recently as 1965, Captain Irving Johnson and his wife Electa gave Society members an account of the country to the south, the ancient land of Nubia. But their voyage in the ketch *Yankee* was a final glimpse of the villages and people here. Joe and I found their Nubia drowning and abandoned.

Within minutes, the northern Sudan slid into view, baked to death even where the Nile brushed orange and black desert. What would we find there that earlier travelers had not seen? From 30,000 feet, we could not tell.

Many things, we knew, remain unchanged from ten years past, or ten centuries. I had read of pyramids by the dozen deep in the Sudan, of camel caravans still jingling over the wasteland. I had read, too, of an astounding journey that touched upon nearly every mile of the Nile. In 1955, the NATIONAL GEOGRAPHIC published the story of a young Californian named John Goddard and his two French companions who traveled from the beginning of the river to the end—mainly in kayaks. Their experiences would guide us. But we would not know the country as a day-to-day experience of our own until we felt the land under our feet.

The southern Sudan appeared, smothered in vibrant green, and there was no Nile—or a thousand Niles lost in swamp. A Roman expedition sent by Nero halted

At the Second Cataract, near the Sudanese-Egyptian border, huge granite boulders once sped the Nile northward. Now the waters of Lake Nasser have blotted out palms and dunes, rocks and rapids.

here, abandoning its quest for the river's source. Arabs stopped too, naming this great marshy expanse "the Barrier." Not until a century ago did men probe farther for the river's beginning: men like Dr. David Livingstone, John Hanning Speke, Richard Francis Burton, Samuel Baker, Henry Morton Stanley, all among the greatest figures of 19th-century exploration.

OUR JET SOARED over Uganda, where the river burrows under jungle and swings through hills as tame and spacious as a park two horizons wide. The plane wheeled over Victoria, Africa's largest lake, and eased down at Entebbe International Airport. We found Paddy O'Reilly there, in the little wooden office of Uganda Aviation Services, Limited. He agreed to fly us as close to the southernmost source of the Nile as a plane can go with any certainty of landing.

Almost every day, Paddy took off from Entebbe, scooting north to pick up a stretcher case, hopping the Congo forest with a cockpit full of diplomats, delivering a businessman to Kenya in the east. Now he calmly picked a path through narrow holes in the tumbling clouds, accustomed to the showery, thundery weather of the east African plateau.

Landing at the little Burundi capital of Bujumbura, Joe and I piled photo gear into a rented station wagon. Early the next morning, the car's owner, Leon Rwabutuna, steered up a twisting mountain road. Low chaotic skies dumped a dozen showers on us every couple of hours. But the red clay track relieved our fears, remaining as hard as pavement.

How many people have traveled to this source of the Nile? Very few, I guessed. Not until 1937 did an obscure German explorer named Dr. Burkhart Waldecker trace the great river to a tiny spring that bubbles up 118 road-miles from Bujumbura. Impoverished and alone, he searched for years. We bumped through damp pastureland for seven hours, straying into wrong turns, jouncing over unmapped trails.

Author Bruce Brander taps the southernmost source of the Nile. A pyramid (right) honoring Nile explorers crowns a Burundi hill nearby. The tiny spring trickles into a ravine, a humble birthplace of the majestic River Nile.

A hundred children squealed and waved, excited to see a car, when we rolled past the red brick school of Rutovu Catholic Mission. A little farther along the road, we stopped at a hill paved with purple flowers. A dozen tribesmen in togas and khaki shorts crowded around the car to see what we would do.

A schoolboy caught up with us, a lad about 14 with the lean face and huge eyes of the Tutsi tribe. He panted a polite *bon jour*, then looked bewildered because we were white men but did not speak fluent French.

He took us in his care anyway, scrambling up a rock and pointing to a small bush-clogged ravine with a certain pride of ownership.

"There," he lectured in his own fluent French, "is the longest river in the world."

NATIONAL GEOGRAPHIC PHOTOGRAPHER JOSEPH J. SCHERSCHEL

2

WATER FOR A GIANT

CAPUT NILI—Source of the Nile. The Latin words, cast in weather-blackened bronze, explained a pyramid that we found on a windy, lonely summit near the Nile's first spring. The small peak of stone was Dr. Waldecker's idea, to mark the spot where the river of the pyramids begins. The inscription he composed for its bronze plaque honors many men of many ages who pondered the vastness of Africa and wondered where this place might be: "Eratosthenes, Ptolemy, Speke, Stanley, Kandt and all the others."

Joe and I decided to honor them with a toast in the first water of the Nile. We hurried down the ravine to a little concrete wall, where a galvanized pipe releases the sparkling spring. Slightly cool, superbly fresh, the water tasted delicious.

A retinue of shepherd boys skipped down the slope behind us and lined up, eager to sip from the spring. Apparently they had never thought of trying it before.

"For how long has this river poured from the pipe?" I asked. "Many years," they answered, but no one knew how many.

Kasumo—cascade—the hill people call the first white plumes that chatter down the slope. Out of sight, Kasumo absorbs many other streams and gets other names, African words that rap and rumble like Burundi drums: Mukasenyi, Kigira, Ruvironza, Ruvubu, Kagera. All of them carry water for the Nile. And all, with occasional turns, flow north.

John Goddard and his companions, Jean Laporte and André Davy, came to Kasumo to begin their journey, but they had to go 200 miles north to the Kagera River for water enough to float their kayaks. Everyone they consulted warned them of rapids on the Kagera, but no one could describe its dangers in detail.

"You chaps are committing triple suicide by kayak," said one worried official.

In the first stretch of white water, they dodged the rocks successfully, and hippos after that. In the second, Goddard's kayak snagged on a root, dragged him along upside down underwater, and he almost drowned. When Davy swerved to pass a hippo, he found his craft sideways at the edge of a cataract in one moment and broken on a rock in another. But they salvaged the boats, made their way through leeches and mosquitoes out of a papyrus swamp, refitted their expedition, and went on.

Going north from Kasumo to other sources of the great river, a more conventional traveler crosses most of Burundi, a kingdom about the size of Maryland, and

Barefoot women of Rwanda, dressed in richly hued *pagnes,* meet on a crumpled volcanic slope on their way to the village well. Lake Kivu sprawls in background. In the hills east of the lake springs the Lukarara River, longest headwater of the Nile.

a slightly smaller country to the north, the Republic of Rwanda. I found them very much the same in many ways.

The land flows north in tall, steep waves. I noticed the absence of trees. Forests could grow here—rain falls abundantly, and lava enriches the soil. But these countries depend on farming, and both are overcrowded with land-hungry people. Here, in the heart of Africa, forests are a luxury, confined mainly to official reserves.

I saw another luxury everywhere: cattle, striking beasts with lyre-shaped horns as long and thick as a man's arms. Munching their living from one-third of the countries' land area, they leave hardly more than hillsides for farming. So people of the Hutu tribe, who work the soil by tradition, have sculpted row after row of earthen terraces along the slopes. The result reminded

Feet stamping and headplumes thrashing, Tutsi warriors prance to the frenetic rhythm of the national dance. Jangling ankle bells accent the staccato clamor of pounding drums. Strands of fiber fringed with colobus monkey fur crown the dancers, and beads cross their chests. Dances of this tribe often mimic the animal kingdom.

NATIONAL GEOGRAPHIC PHOTOGRAPHER JOSEPH J. SCHERSCHEL

Wistful-eyed Tutsi carries a sample of her weaving, a craft mastered by women of this advanced tribe. Features of the Tutsi, descendants of an early Bahima tribe, reflect an original Hamite stock now mixed with dark-skinned peoples.

W. ROBERT MOORE, NATIONAL GEOGRAPHIC STAFF

me of an undulating staircase, leading up, then down, for miles in every direction.

In this panorama of green and tan stripes, I could hardly discern the farmers, all lost in natural camouflage. Some drift like languid swimmers through a green river of maize stalks. Others bend low to hoe bean patches, shouting conversations over nearby fields of peas, sorghum, cassava.

When we met them along the road, the Hutu stood out clearly enough: stocky, muscular, broad-shouldered people. A sturdy folk, they reminded me of Bavarian farmers from deep among the Alps.

All over the hills, I saw feathers of white smoke rising as farmers burned agricultural waste. Thin clouds of kitchen smoke also intrigued me. When the women cook inside their thatched huts, the roofs appear to be steaming.

These huts poke up among the crops like haystacks, each with a patch of bananas around it. Every family grows its own food, and brews its own beer from banana pulp. And the cash crop? From a distance, it seemed the gentler slopes were planted with red confetti: coffee berries, the main export of both Burundi and Rwanda. But neither country has much coffee, or much cash; only three percent of all the farmland grows a money crop.

"With just a few more acres . . ." the local dream begins. But a shrug shoves the vision away. "The cattle must eat too."

Foreign visitors often wonder why these cattle must eat—or exist, for that matter. Undernourished for lack of ample pasture, a typical cow yields very little milk. Herd owners forbid anyone to use an animal for meat and leather until it dies of age or sickness. So the longhorned pets—more than a million of them—keep five million people on the edge of famine, giving almost nothing in return.

Almost nothing, I mean, except prestige. Here, as elsewhere in Africa, a man has few delights greater than title to a great herd. Cattle give him status, wealth, security—and the longer the horns, the greater the prize.

"But why cattle?" a traveler might ask.

"Why gold? Why diamonds?" a farmer will reply with reasonable logic and a glance at the stranger's ring finger.

As we drove along, Leon would point to a cow and rattle off the price it might bring. A good one might fetch 5,000 to 6,000 Burundi francs—say, $65.

JUST AS CATTLE might buy a hut or a secondhand car today, they once bought much of the Nile's sourceland. About the time Europeans were migrating to colonies in America, tall herdsmen of the Hamitic race were driving their four-legged wealth along a southwest arc across Africa. The lean nomads originated in Ethiopia, most authorities believe. Their cattle represented an ancient strain, resembling the longhorned bulls that stride in stone across some Egyptian ruins.

Some of these nomads stopped in the southern Sudan and Uganda. Others pushed on to the cool green slopes of Rwanda and Burundi. Here Hutu tribesmen, part of the great Bantu family, were already farming the hills. Instead of arguing over the land, it appears that the two peoples came to an agreement, a strange social arrangement that reminds me of Tom Sawyer's fence-painting deal.

Barricade of horns blocks a Uganda highway as Ankole cattle plod to pasture. Lyre-horned

The Hutu admired the tall newcomers and their animals; they would labor for the herdsmen if only the herdsmen would let them take care of the splendid cattle. This put the cattle-rich nomads on the royal road to dominance. A feudal system called *ubuhake* spread over the land and solidified. The Hutu became serfs, caring for the cattle and performing most manual chores; the herd owners, known by the tribal name of Tutsi, became overlords.

At the turn of the century, the two countries formed part of German East Africa, but local ways changed little. In 1923, a League of Nations mandate left the region in Belgian hands, and Belgium governed it as a single colony, Ruanda-Urundi. Still, each section kept its Tutsi *mwami,* or king, and the cattle-owning Tutsi chiefs continued to dominate the Hutu.

The rulers, better known abroad as the Watutsi, have fascinated foreigners. They are among the giants of the continent, rod-straight and aristocratic. Not all Tutsi stand as tall as foreigners expect; they average five feet nine inches. But men rising seven feet six are not uncommon. Even perched on a bicycle, with a vassal pushing, a Tutsi is an elegant sight.

I could often recognize the Tutsi at a glance. Their faces are lean and triangular, their great eyes round and wistful. They look frail; they carry themselves with the grace of ballet dancers, gliding rather than walking, moving like wisps of dark smoke.

In centuries of leisure, the Tutsi raised local arts to a high level. A rural noble may brighten the walls of his hut with finely woven tapestries of dyed banana fiber. He may sit at ease for hours while an *inanga,* a kind of zither, fills the air with a mist of music. But he admires dancing above all other art forms.

Anyone who sees a Tutsi dance puts it away with the unforgettable sights of life. Great drums, each half the height of a man, blast like cannonfire—slowly at first, faster to raise the gooseflesh, deeper to a steady hypnotic rumble. Drummers squeeze their eyes shut and leap in a swirl of red and white cloth. Lean dancers in leopard skins and ankle bells prance and writhe, swishing

cows carved on Egyptian monuments suggest present-day beasts descend from an ancient breed.

GILBERT H. GROSVENOR

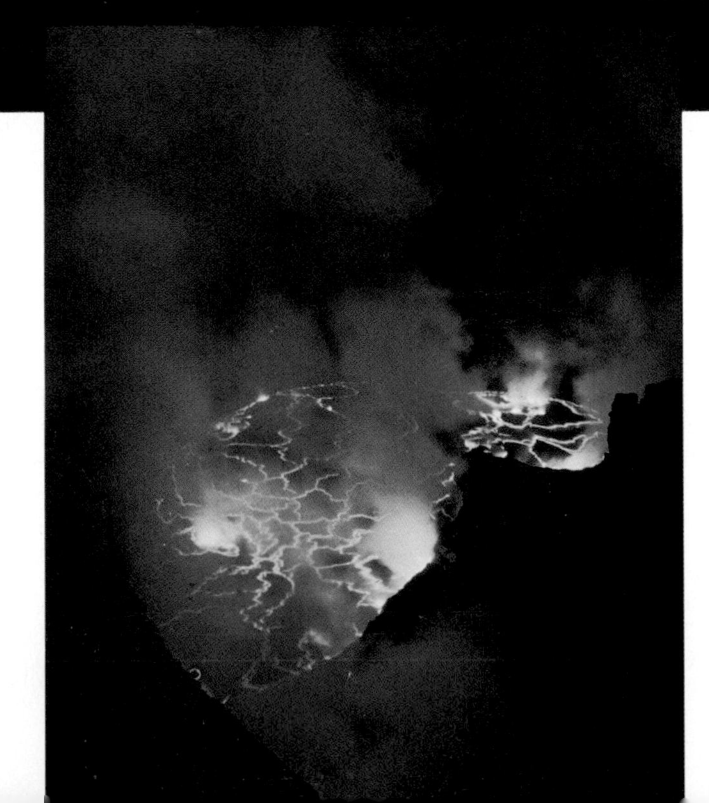

Blue mist of dawn tints Lake Mutanda in southwest Uganda. Beyond the shore dormant volcanic triplets rise in the Virunga range, home of the mountain gorilla and part of the Nile's watershed. Mount Muhavura (left), Mount Gahinga (center), and ragged Sabinyo cross the Rift Valley.

Nyiragongo, one of Virunga's two active volcanoes, rises in the Democratic Republic of the Congo. The cone's magma lake (left) simmers at 1,470° F. Local legend says Nyiragongo bears the name of a tribeswoman whose spirit haunts the area.

PAUL A. ZAHL, NATIONAL GEOGRAPHIC STAFF (ABOVE), AND EMIL SCHULTHESS, BLACK STAR

long staffs in front of them. Their leaps are phenomenal, and flopping headdresses of white colobus monkey fur make them seem higher still.

In days past, Tutsi dances represented war: *Umuheto, Icumu, Ingabo,* the tribesmen called them, "the Bow, the Lance, the Shield." Now, the violent motion tells of "the Marvelous" and "the Female-provoker," and other dances say "Thanks" and "That puts an end to all discussion."

Can feudalism survive in a time of worldwide social revolution? In 1954, Belgian administrators in Ruanda-Urundi decided it was dangerous, at best. And at worst? They tried to prevent the worst. That year, they issued a decree requiring chiefs to give two-thirds of their cattle to serfs who tended the herds. For a while, the law seemed to work. But the Tutsi resented the new order, just as the Hutu had come to resent the old.

A turning point for half the region came in 1959, when Ruanda's mwami died. Before the new king came to power, the Hutu rebelled. They outnumbered their Tutsi overlords six to one, and soon overpowered the aristocrats.

July, 1962, brought independence to both countries. Ruanda became the Republic of Rwanda. While its Hutu ministers went about their duties in economy cars and patched clothing, thousands of its Tutsi citizens smouldered in exile. Urundi

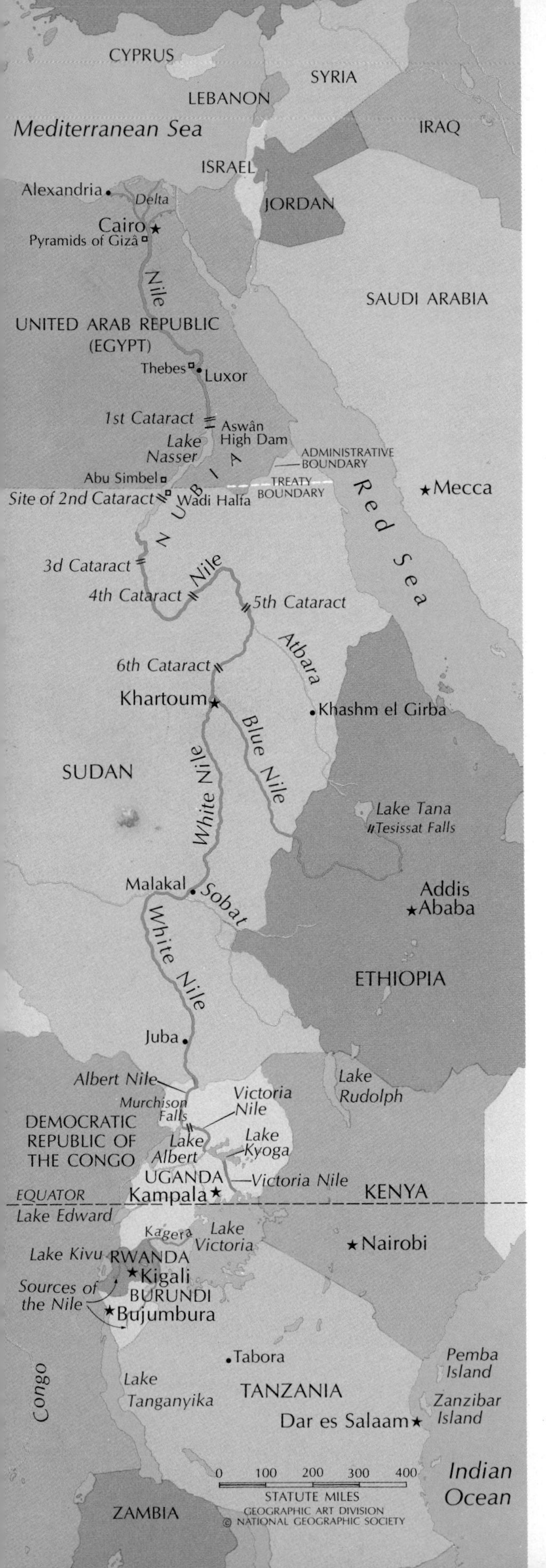

added a capital B to its name and remained a kingdom—and a sanctuary for many of the refugees.

Inyenzi—cockroaches—exiled Tutsi warriors are called, because they strike at night. Several times since Independence Day, inyenzi have swarmed through the hills of Rwanda, showering their former serfs with spears and arrows, hoping to recover the land they lost, the cattle, serfs, and status. Once they crept within 12 miles of Rwanda's little capital city, Kigali, before the Republic's army drove them back with automatic weapons.

The terrified government of Rwanda sometimes took revenge. In 1963 and 1964, more than 10,000 Tutsi men, women and children were killed. But the proud, shrewd aristocrats allow none of their number to surrender. Whenever a Tutsi refugee plants a banana tree—a symbol of permanent residence—inyenzi emerge at night to cut it down.

The Nile runs everywhere through these two lands, in streams that furrow the hills with bright fresh water. But some sources are more significant than others. Rwanda's Lukarara River, for example, is the longest headwater. From its tip in the nation's far west, mapmakers begin to measure the Nile's 4,145-mile length. Eventually, all these streams meet, mix, and pour into the huge basin of Lake Victoria. There ends one of the Nile's great source systems. Not far away, another one begins—a chain of mountains and lakes some 300 miles long.

Very early in the morning, mist hides the peaks of the Virunga range. The road leads out of the northwest corner of Rwanda into the Democratic Republic of the Congo. Eight volcanoes, all more than 10,000 feet high, rise ahead, curving as serenely as ocean swells. As the soft haze lifts, hundreds of smaller cones appear among them,

World's longest river, the Nile stretches like a lifeline through Africa for 4,145 miles. At Khartoum in the Sudan, the Blue Nile, streaking from Lake Tana in Ethiopia, merges with the White Nile that first trickles in Rwanda and Burundi. From Khartoum they surge as one commanding current to the Mediterranean.

Rwanda mother, one of millions of persons depending on Nile waters, grinds grain as she holds her child in an *ingobyi,* a leather sling.

COURTESY AMERICAN MUSEUM OF NATURAL HISTORY

Potbellied monster, this 360-pound gorilla, nearly six feet tall, once shuffled through the highland bush of central Africa. Hunter Herbert Bradley (right) shot the mountain giant in 1921. Naturalist Carl Akeley, next to Mrs. Bradley, cups the gaping jaw.

cracked off at the top like soft-boiled eggs.

Karisimbi, highest of the range, sometimes collects snow on its 14,787-foot summit. The Twa clans of the region, a people related to the pygmies, say it collects something better; they believe that good souls go there, to a dazzling heaven.

Their hell is Nyiragongo, a live volcano that much of the time lies misleadingly quiescent, huffing out lazy wisps of yellow smoke. But periodically it and another peak called Nyamulagira thunder back into action. One eruption not long ago gushed a fan of white-hot lava six miles wide, 14 miles long. Strangely, a fiery river such as this adds volume to the Nile. Clouds bunch together, heavy and low over the molten flow, later releasing their moisture in rain.

Where lava has not scarred it, the Virunga country is green with jungle. "Stop!" a guide may whisper in these forests, and a traveler will wait in tense silence while an elephant herd blocks the track ahead. The range rolls deep into the Kivu National Park, so leopards, hyenas, forest hogs, and buffalo may wander along the path.

Mountain gorillas live on the slopes of an extinct volcano called Mikeno. From a distance, this mountain looks like an old Prussian army helmet, rising steeply, ending in a point. But on the walls of Mt. Mikeno, thick stalks and broad leaves close in tightly and screen the summit from view. This is the weird world of the bamboo forest, sunless, misty green. The air smells like freshly peeled twigs. Moss wipes against the skin, wet and cold.

The gorillas of these clammy slopes are among the rarest animals on earth. Scientists distinguish them from their lowland cousins, known by the monotonous Latin name *Gorilla gorilla gorilla.* This mountain breed, called *Gorilla gorilla beringei,* runs slightly smaller, standing under six feet, weighing less than 500 pounds. And heavier fur guards them against the cold.

Their shyness works against your chance of meeting one in the forests of Mt. Mikeno. Unless angered, a gorilla rarely attacks. He could wrench the head off a man with ease, or buckle a gun barrel between his teeth. But, as the American naturalist Carl Akeley put it, ". . . the gorilla is normally a perfectly amiable and decent creature." He would rather scramble away than fight.

A river named Rwindi carries much of the Virunga rainwater out of the range and into Lake Edward. The oval lake, almost 50 miles long, got its name in the 1880's, honoring Britain's future King Edward VII. But I prefer its simple, more descriptive nickname, "the bird lake."

Colonies of pelicans glide like feathered dreadnoughts over quiet southern inlets. Flamingos step daintily among them. In the thick, soft haze that hangs over the water during part of the year, egrets and fish martins appear and race, gulls plunge at fish, and Nile geese flutter from marshes along the shore.

On firmer land, hippopotamuses by the thousand loaf like monstrous sea slugs. Farther inland rove wart hogs, antelopes, elephants, and lions.

People of the area, forbidden to kill game, fish for their living. They reap great harvests of perch, tigerfish, and mudfish from Lake Edward, and greater ones from the tiny Lake George just next door. Dugout canoes and aluminum boats skim to the shores loaded with slippery silver. Modern processing plants take over from there.

At the north end of Lake Edward, waters for the Nile pour into the Semliki River. This stream swings widely through Congo territory, over rapids and falls, past dense jungle. If you follow the Semliki to the end, you come to Lake Albert, which sends all its waters on the journey toward Egypt. Far better, though, to stop along the way, for this river is passing the great and legendary mountains of the Nile's sourcelands.

NO ONE lives in the Mountains of the Moon. Ba'amba and Bakonjo tribesmen hunt in the foothills, but only a few scientists go higher, or adventurous mountaineers who want to crunch over equatorial snow.

Ridiculous! said London's geographical experts in 1848, when they heard of glaciered African mountains. Captured moonlight, said local tribes. Salt, reasoned an African boy who passed the Mountains of the Moon in 1888 with the first modern explorer to see them. The American journalist Henry M. Stanley was leading this expedition; at first glance, he thought the icy crags were swirls of white mist in the stormy sky. Later, he wrote: "Peak after peak struggled from behind night-black clouds, . . . immense and beautiful."

Stanley used the native name for the range—Ruwenzori, or Rainmaker. He chose well. Clouds bundle over it more

(Continued on page 32)

GEORGE B. SCHALLER

Under a tree-top canopy, young gorillas perch in the rain forest on slopes of the Virunga volcanoes. Adults of this rare mountain species, *Gorilla gorilla beringei,* reach such cumbersome weight that they seldom climb trees. These anthropoids relish the tender pith of banana stems, and to obtain the food they often raid local plantations.

Snow on the Equator: Ice sheets cap the brooding Mountains of the Moon that thrust thousands of feet above the borders of Uganda and the Congo. Giant candelabra of groundsels (foreground) branch below the cloud-clad Ruwenzori range.

PAUL A. ZAHL, NATIONAL GEOGRAPHIC STAFF

2/3 LIFE SIZE; PAUL A. ZAHL, NATIONAL GEOGRAPHIC STAFF

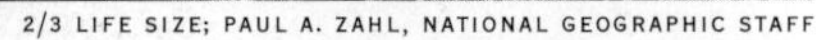

1/3 LIFE SIZE; EMIL SCHULTHESS, BLACK STAR

Bizarre flora and fauna of the eerie Ruwenzori: Like flames of fire, petals of a *Gloriosa* (above) ignite the dank jungle heights with color. This lilylike climber thrives at an altitude of 6,800 feet. Candlelike blossoms (left) sprout from the spike of a *wollastonii* lobelia. In these weird regions, some plants soar three times as tall as man. This gigantism stems from cool climate, acid soil, and intense ultraviolet light, scientists suggest. About A.D. 150 Ptolemy called this unearthly region the Mountains of the Moon. Tribesmen in the area named the range Ruwenzori, or Rainmaker, because of its constant brooding weather. Oddest creature in these alpine heights and distant cousin of the elephant, a hyrax (left) crouches among boulders. Called a "rock rabbit," this strange button-nosed mammal has hoofs instead of claws, and shrills a sound like a whistle. A member of the genus *Procavia,* the hyrax makes a tasty dish when boiled with a pinch of salt. An expedition (opposite) from Makerere College in Uganda trudges up moss-slick slopes from Lake Bujuku (far left) below Mount Baker.

1/7 LIFE SIZE; NORMAN R. LIGHTFOOT, PHOTO RESEARCHERS

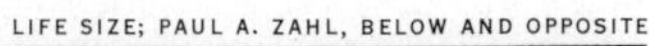

LIFE SIZE; PAUL A. ZAHL, BELOW AND OPPOSITE

Scaly skin and spurlike horns give *Chamaeleo johnstoni* (right) a prehistoric look. Local tribesmen refuse to touch the chameleon, believing it an evil omen. The heavy-lidded eyes of the five-inch reptile swivel in revolving sockets.

than 300 days of the year, and the range is one of the wettest on earth. But it still keeps the name Ptolemy, the Alexandrian geographer, put on his map, about A.D. 150, *Lunae Montes,* "Mountains of the Moon."

A journey to the glaciers that feed the Nile takes about five days from Fort Portal, Uganda, near the Congo border. You go on foot, with porters, supplies, and guides.

Nearly every valley of the Ruwenzori is soggy with silt, and feet seem twice as heavy as usual as they slog through the swampland. Grass thrives here, swaying in the mist, as high as healthy corn and twice as dense. The porters are hushed—elephants and buffalo may amble along these trails, up the slopes through bracken and nettles. Both animals roam as high as 5,500 feet.

A thousand feet higher, a new vegetation zone begins, the second of six that grow progressively colder as the track leads from the tropical base to glacial summits. Nervous porters may build a shrine of twigs here, and offer little piles of sugar to spirits of the region. They feel better with the spirits on their side just now. Lions and wild pigs prowl the next 2,000 feet of altitude. Leopards climb all the way to the snowline.

THE LITTLE CARAVAN of porters moves like a caterpillar through *Cyathea* tree ferns, wild bananas, and evergreen trees. Then come bamboo forests. The thick stalks grow 12 to 20 inches every day. They creak overhead 40, 60, 100 feet off the ground.

When evening comes, porters set up camp and carefully lay snares around it, hoping to catch a monkey or a small serval cat. With greater luck, they will get a hyrax. This peculiar animal makes a sound like a whistle and looks like a rabbit. But it walks on hoofs and is distantly related to the elephant and the rhinoceros. The porters boil it with a pinch of salt, and consider it quite tasty.

The morning chill lasts all day when the expedition gets above 10,000 feet. And here begins the country scientists come to see. In this dank and misty land, nature goes wild. Tall growths slither upward, shaggy black trunks fully sturdy as trees. "They're groundsel, *Senecio,*" a botanist will point out; "you know, the stuff that comes in little bunches for canary food." The canary-food weeds, a foot high in other parts of the world, loom in the fog as tall as telephone poles.

Canaries 15 feet from beak to tail would not astonish you here. Earthworms grow three feet long. Pretty little flowers of temperate gardens have moon-mountain cousins ten feet tall. Scotsmen, who say white heather means good fortune, can stroll 32 feet deep in luck.

What produces these giants? Eternal dampness, cold, intense ultraviolet rays, and acid soil rich in minerals, botanists suggest. But no one knows for certain.

Porters do not want to know much about *Chamaeleo johnstoni.* A few years ago, Dr. Paul A. Zahl, NATIONAL GEOGRAPHIC natural scientist, offered a reward to his men for one of these scaly reptiles. He did not get one. The Bakonjo say the five-inch monster is a crawling omen of evil. They selected an appropriate goblin—three ugly horns poke directly out of its face.

Gold and green moss borders the trail, a musty vegetable sponge waist-deep in places. Higher still, the path leads past marshes and brilliantly colored lakes into low brush as thick and green as lawn.

When the air gets thin and climbers begin to feel the nausea and headache of mountain sickness, the world around is a wild fantasy. Clouds swirl above and below. Cliffs plunge away into fog. Streams hurtle into space and blow in the wind like shredded silk. The pinnacles are just above, higher than the highest Alps of Europe. Vittorio Emanuele rises 16,042 feet; Alexandra is higher; Margherita towers above them all at 16,763 feet.

A cosy refuge hut stands here for anyone who needs it. As soon as food and blankets are unpacked, someone will build a fire. By late afternoon, temperatures fall well below freezing here on the Equator. As the cabin gets warm, the windows get steamy. A traveler has to rub a peephole to see the Ruwenzori's glacial source of the Nile. Not far away, waters that will slip through jungles, tropical swamps, and deserts wait in bright ice-cliffs for the next day's sun to melt them.

Like a spray of bursting fireworks, the flowers of a poker plant *(Kniphofia)* blaze atop a thick treelike stem. Members of the bulb-sprouting lily family, some 70 species of this perennial herb shoot up in central and south Africa.

Robt. Atkinson

3

DISCOVERY

OLD CHIEF BAGAYA had a lot to say. *Uhuru*—freedom—came to most of the Nile's sourceland that year, 1962. People of Uganda bought ties and dresses in national colors. Crowds in Rwanda danced the "Independence Cha Cha Cha." In Burundi, where the old chief lived, Belgians watched and 20,000 Africans cheered; a new flag went up over Usumbura, the capital, later renamed Bujumbura. It was a year of elation and high hopes. But Chief Bagaya, reminiscing to reporters, had his mind on distant days and another independence.

"We thought they were freaks, or animals," he said, recalling invaders who had defied the kingdom's borders. They wrapped their legs in cloth. They rode on the backs of beasts. And their skins were white. What could the warriors do? The old Tutsi leader remembered. "Our chief got us all together and we decided to attack these strange animals."

In 1962, Chief Bagaya believed he was about a century old. He said he remembered the day in 1871 when Stanley found Dr. Livingstone, about a mile from the chief's home. He could picture the peculiar horse-borne "animals" in gaiters who met the attacking tribesmen with guns—Germans, following in the wake of explorers, seeking new colonies.

Traders, armies, trains, and cities... neon, bombs, and bulldozers—it was quite a century for Chief Bagaya.

For east Africa, the astounding century began a half-dozen years or so before the old chief was born. In 1856, two Englishmen landed on the Island of Zanzibar in the Indian Ocean, 20 miles off Africa's coast.

Then as now, Arabs, Persians, Swahilis, Indians, and other traders from all over the world crowded the streets of Zanzibar City. Then, as now, they dealt in cloves. But then they dealt, too, in exotic treasures brought in caravans from unmapped, unknown depths of Africa.

Rhinoceros horn for the Orient? Ivory for Europe? Slaves for the courts and harems of Arabia? Zanzibar bazaars had plenty. What better place to begin a quest for the source of the Nile than here, at the start of Africa's mysterious trading trail?

Slave and ivory caravans counted on at least one year inland. John Hanning Speke allowed for two. This tall, slender, blond Englishman had been planning the journey for a long time. During ten army years in India, he toughened himself with hunting trips to unexplored Himalaya country. He never, as he later wrote, idled away his time or got into debt. Methodical and

Goal for centuries: British explorer John Hanning Speke (seated) maps the river he found rushing over Ripon Falls from a lake he named for Queen Victoria in 1862. The river must be the Nile, he wrote, the lake its major source.

determined, he lived soberly and saved his money. In 1854, he took a three-year leave and set out for the lands where the Nile had its legendary source.

He was sidetracked immediately. Speke's ship put in at Aden. There he met an adventurer already famous, Richard Francis Burton, now bound for the wild mountainous interior of Abyssinia.

The 33-year-old Burton, Speke's elder by almost six years, was a fascinating man. Tall, muscular, intelligent, he could tell of India's bazaars where he had roamed in Oriental robes and dyed face, of Mecca, Islam's forbidden city, which he had entered and lived to describe. And all the while his "panther eyes" would stare from a proud, sinister, melancholy face. Speke turned away from the Nile and joined Burton.

NOT UNTIL two years later did the two men land in Zanzibar. Their Abyssinian notes had been published, their spear wounds had healed, and Britain's Royal Geographical Society was sponsoring Burton's journey, this time into the equatorial unknown. Speke had the Nile on his mind again.

"People here tell frightful stories about the dangers and difficulty of the journey," Burton wrote to the Society's secretary, "and I don't believe a word of it."

Still, they prepared well. They packed swords, rifles, revolvers, and enough ammunition for two years. For comfort, they included a tent, portable table, chairs, mattresses, blankets, mosquito netting, pillows, and carpet mats. They had tools for blacksmithing and carpentry, wrapped in bundles. They carried compasses, chronometers, thermometers, sextants, a barometer, a portable sundial, a table of the stars, and a set of miscellaneous books, including Galton's *Art of Travel.*

Hunting and barter would provide food along the way. But they took a supply of tea, coffee, salt, spices, pepper, pickles, brandy, soap, snuff, and cigars.

With special care they chose an assortment of beads from some 400 varieties. As Burton later explained in a highly detailed book, the cheapest ones were the "Ushanga Waupe, a round white porcelain." The costliest were called "Kimara-p'hamba (food-finishers), because a man will part

(Continued on page 40)

FREELANCE PHOTOGRAPHERS GUILD (ABOVE), HARRISON FORMAN (LOWER LEFT), AND PIP PHOTOS, INC.

Tossing spices, rice, herbs, and *ghee* to feed the fire in an ancient Hindu ceremony called *Havan*, worshipers recite Sanskrit prayers, psalm-like verses praising the wind, sunrise, and the heavens. The devout observe this rite twice daily and on special occasions such as marriages. North of Dar es Salaam, home of these celebrants and capital of Tanzania, slave caravans of the 1800's departed for Africa's interior.

Nineteenth-century explorers once bargained with merchants in the narrow streets of exotic Zanzibar City (left). The Island of Zanzibar became a base for expeditions bound for the unknown African heartland.

Following the text with his hand, a Zanzibar merchant reads the Koran in front of his shop. Most Zanzibaris are Sunni Moslems, the most numerous of Islamic sects. Islam means "surrender to God's will."

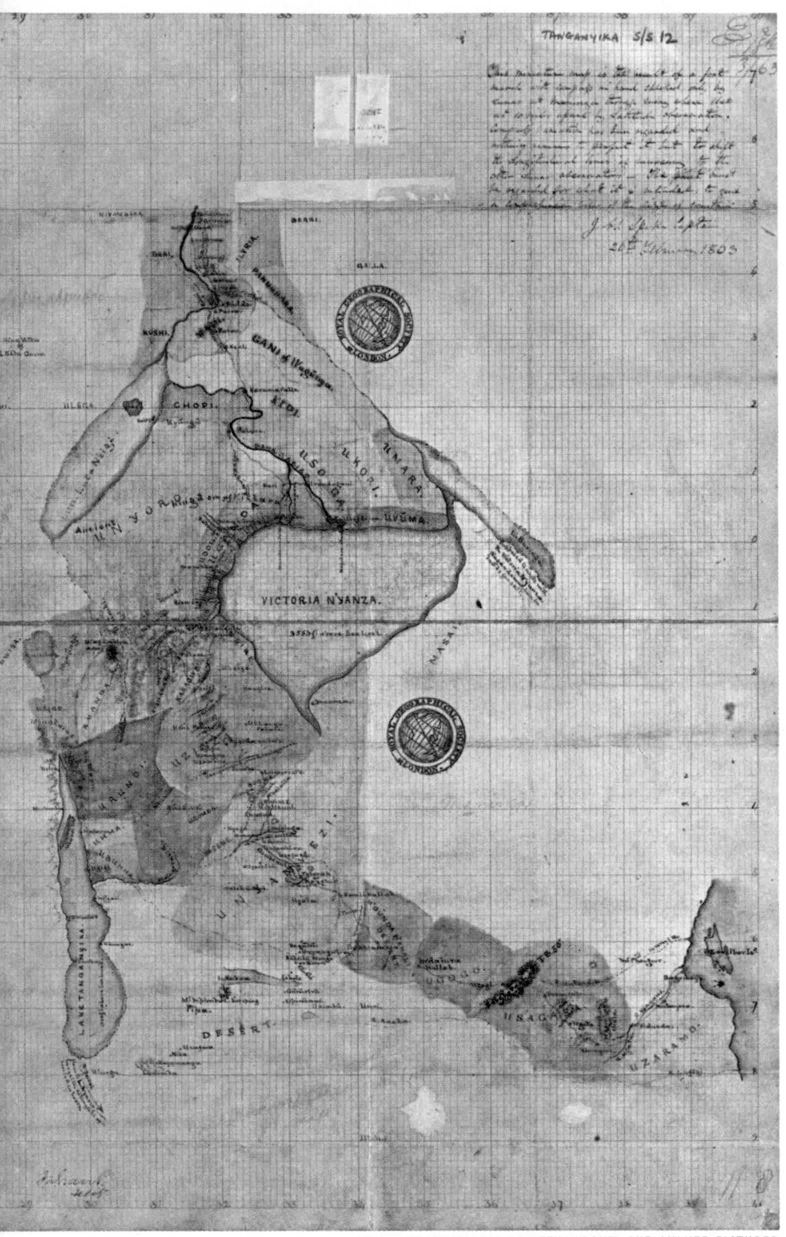

ROYAL GEOGRAPHICAL SOCIETY (ABOVE) AND CULVER PICTURES

With a compass, a sextant, and a watch, Speke and Grant mapped the lake region of central Africa, then a mysterious, forbidding area. Speke's note in the upper right corner explains that this "miniature map" gives "a comprehensive view" of the countries they visited. Most of the boundaries shown no longer concern cartographers, but "Urundi" and "Ruanda" appear as Burundi and Rwanda on today's maps. Grant used "*N'yanza,*" the Bantu word "lake," for Victoria. To show that he drew this map, Grant added the Latin *fecit* [he made it] after his signature in the lower left corner.

Pomp of courtly ritual unfolds

Iron-willed partners: John Hanning Speke and James Augustus Grant set out in 1860 to establish Lake Victoria as the Nile's source. Illness halted Grant (right); Speke pressed on to find the Nile emerging from the lake's northern rim.

Dashing adventurer: Richard Francis Burton (opposite) and Speke teamed up in 1858 to explore central Africa and search for the Nile's source. They failed to find it, but Burton recorded valuable knowledge of the continent.

efore Speke and Grant at a levee given in their honor by Mutesa I, King of Buganda.

FROM "JOURNAL OF THE DISCOVERY OF THE SOURCE OF THE NILE" BY J. H. SPEKE, 1863, (BELOW) AND CULVER PICTURES

ROLAND EITH, KEYSTONE PRESS

with his dinner to obtain them, and Kifunjyá-mji (town-breakers), because the women will ruin themselves and their husbands for them; these are the small coral-bead, scarlet enamelled upon a white ground. . . ." Africans, he said, would disdain gold and silver, but never beads.

He listed other trade goods—brass wire and a cloth called "'*merkani,*' in which we detect the African corruption of American . . . unbleached shirting and sheeting from the mills near Salem." Their caravan started inland in June, 1857. Tanzania's central railway follows the old slave and ivory route in a general way. The caravans started from Bagamoyo; the railroad begins some 45 miles south, at the port of Dar es Salaam. The train clatters over a coastal belt through liquid green coconut plantations. At first the air feels like damp velvet on your skin, but the moist wind of the Indian Ocean soon lags behind.

Miles of sisal cover the land like crew-cut hair. The tracks flash into lonely country of low limestone ridges, thornbushes, and baobab trees with fat tubs for trunks and antlers for branches. Even clicking along steel rails, you can see Burton's noisy,

PIP PHOTOS, INC. (ABOVE) AND EMIL SCHULTHESS, BLACK STAR

Sisal leaves bristle from a field in Tanzania, source of a third of the world's supply. Today's annual production of more than 200,000 tons started from an experimental planting of 62 bulbs in 1892. Swaying like dancers, young girls (left) carry dried sisal to balers. Strong and flexible, sisal ranks second only to Manila hemp in the manufacture of cordage.

Barrel-shaped baobab tree lifts fanlike branches toward a luminous African sky. Some tribesmen hollow out the trunks of these trees—many of them 30 feet in girth—for houses or to fashion wells for water storage. "... the devil plucked up the baobab," Arabian legend says, "thrust its branches into the earth, and left its roots in air."

scattered caravan. He rides a donkey. His Goanese servant, Valentine, plods nearby. Speke rides too, though at least once he strode barefoot to toughen body and spirit. With them are 129 other marchers.

Personal slaves attend many of the caravan guards, who trudge along with muzzle-loaders and German cavalry sabers. The porters go armed too, and their women and children clap and shout to keep cattle and goats in line.

The donkeys—about 30 of them at first—scuff along docilely for a while, but then one kicks and they all bolt, veer, and break out of file. The procession halts. *"Unká nám gadha!"* shrieks Valentine—"Their name *is* jackass!"—and half a dozen porters drop their bundles to hold the animals and rope the loads in place for the third or fourth time since five o'clock that morning.

Somebody waves and the march resumes. A guide leads, with the sagging red flag of Zanzibar. A drummer struts behind. Everybody is singing, whistling, and yelling to warn nearby tribes that this is a mighty caravan, not to be attacked.

But might melted into prudence when the marchers met a band of young Wazaramo warriors, "grasping in one hand their full-sized bows, and in the other sheaths of grinded arrows, whose black barbs and necks showed a fresh layer of poison." Their chief wanted *"kuhonga"*—a toll of beads and wire and cloth. Sometimes explorers would haggle for hours, perhaps days, over these tolls before they could cross tribal lands.

Trade goods paid their way through jungle, plains, and swamps, sometimes all three in a single day's march between five and eleven in the morning. In the afternoon, when they felt well enough, Burton and Speke took notes, sketched, hired local tribesmen to replace porters who had deserted. Often, they were not well. Malaria, pleurisy, ophthalmia, pneumonia, dysentery, and ulcerated sores weakened them.

But only a camp epidemic could quell the dancing when the moon was up. Burton recorded these nights. Sometimes one man, a buffoon, would begin, hurling himself around in the silver glow. Then the porters circled the fire, one singing, others humming, swaying, stamping. They swayed faster, stamped harder, arms shot out and thrashed, bodies writhed, and they jammed together into one tight, twitching clump.

"When the fun threatens to become too fast and furious," Burton wrote, "the song dies, and the performers, with loud shouts of laughter, throw themselves on the ground. 'Nice! nice! very nice!'" old men would applaud. About eight o'clock the camp slipped into silence, women whispering, dull red fires flaring against the jungle, sometimes distant drums mumbling about feast or war.

IF YOU GET OFF THE TRAIN TODAY, at Gulwe, perhaps, and strike out to the north, you will see something of what Speke and Burton found.

Slavery? Old men have tales of that; it persisted in Tanganyika even after the law forbade it. Arab traders? Now they deal in cloth and illegal rhinoceros horn instead of slaves. Fighting? Newspapers tell of a tribal feud or a young hotblood who has staggered to a bush doctor with a poisoned arrow in his side. And animals? You can see those from the train itself, in the land of wide horizons where zebras and giraffes rumble through clouds of red dust.

For almost five months Burton's clamorous caravan yelled and whistled over the empty sprawl of east Africa. Their red flag led them across the Great Rift Valley. But they made slow progress; a hard day's march might take them only four or five miles. On November 7, 1857, they paraded into Kazeh, with "booming horns, muskets ringing like saluting mortars, and an uproar of voices."

The city there today, 529 miles by rail from Dar es Salaam, is called Tabora. Train lines and an airport make it a busy commercial hub for western Tanzania. Time has crumbled the mud-walled *tembes* of Arab traders, quite large homes with courtyards, slave quarters, and harems. White ants have twice destroyed reproductions of the house where the American journalist Henry M. Stanley and Dr. David Livingstone lived in 1872, after their historic meeting. Now the government has rebuilt it in concrete block.

For a month Speke and Burton rested here, questioning Arabs about the country beyond. In December, they headed westward again.

The main rail line, finished in 1914, roughly traces their route for 251 miles

"Dr. Livingstone, I presume," Henry M. Stanley (left) greets David Livingstone upon their historic meeting on November 10, 1871, at Ujiji on the shore of Lake Tanganyika. Two years earlier James Gordon Bennett, manager of the *New York Herald,* had hired Stanley to find the long-missing doctor and missionary turned explorer. Livingstone searched too far south for the source of the Nile; worn by years of hardship in the African bush, he died without attaining his goal.

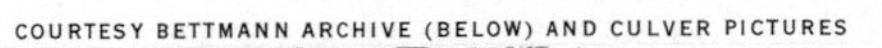

COURTESY BETTMANN ARCHIVE (BELOW) AND CULVER PICTURES

VOLKMAR WENTZEL, NATIONAL GEOGRAPHIC STAFF

to Kigoma, on Lake Tanganyika. The tracks end there, but a short drive south takes you to Ujiji, once an ivory and slaving center. Here the two Englishmen triumphantly reached a great central lake.

Was this vast reservoir the birthplace of the Nile? They crept north in dugout canoes to find out.

At the lake's northern tip, they learned that it was not. A river called Ruzizi flowed south, into the lake—it could not be the Nile. "I felt sick at heart," Burton wrote later. In one of the minor ironies of history, they came within 60 miles of Dr. Waldecker's southernmost source of the Nile, as they paddled over Lake Tanganyika. Yet even if they had found it, they could hardly have recognized Kasumo as the Nile, among Burundi's countless rivulets.

Besides, Speke and Burton wanted the grand, legendary sources: the Mountains

With deadpan dignity, a giraffe, tallest of all the mammals, surveys its domain from a height of 16 feet. Violently swinging their long necks, males use their horns to spar with rival bulls. In Speke and Burton's day, these stilt-legged giants roamed African plains in great numbers. Today only a fraction of their breed survives.

"The terror of the villagers," Speke said of the leopard. A lone hunter, it often ambushes its prey from a tree, dragging the kill back into the branches to elude scavengers.

Kicking up clouds of dust, zebras gallop across open grassland. Some experts believe that stripes may help moderate the zebra's body temperature in the scorching African sun, the black streaks absorbing the heat and the white areas reflecting it.

DAVID GOODNOW (ABOVE) AND ELIOT ELISOFON, COURTESY LIFE MAGAZINE

of the Moon, and a huge reservoir lake. With all the blank sprawl of the dark continent around them, Kasumo would not have been enough. By June, 1858, they were back at Kazeh. They had been on the march for a year.

The *nyanza* to the north is bigger than your lake, Tabora traders assured them. Burton wanted to refit the caravan and compile notes on the nyanza already discovered. But Speke, with porters and guards, went north to see if he could indeed find a bigger lake than Tanganyika.

The present northward road streaks over Tanzania like a bullwhip. Villagers dart about the country in the dry season, touching torches to the grass, so newly blackened earth will send up green shoots for their cattle. Farther on lies the Williamson Diamond Mine, then a landscape broken with granite outcrops, and swamps screaming with birds.

THE AIR begins to change, newly moist, smelling like spring rain. *Cassia* trees border the road; beyond spread fields of rice, cotton, peanuts, millet. After 224 miles the road ends at Mwanza, on the shores of Africa's greatest lake.

Here Speke's questions ended in certainty. "I no longer felt any doubt," he wrote, "that the lake at my feet gave birth to that interesting river, the source of which has been the subject of so much speculation, and the object of so many explorers."

In the evening, you can see Lake Victoria as he did—the shore sparkling with fireflies, islands sprawling like monstrous crocodiles. When the moon is high at night, drums might begin; they carry far, because the lake is almost as large as the Republic of Ireland.

Guesswork, Burton protested when Speke returned. How could anyone assume the Nile flowed from the north end of a lake, when he stood at the south end and admittedly did not see across it? Burton had a point, of course. But Speke would not concede it. The two men, exhausted, ill, and exasperated with each other, trekked away to the coast and sailed for England.

Nearly two years later, Speke set out again. This time he had the patronage of the Royal Geographical Society. With him went another English officer, the 34-year-old Capt. James Augustus Grant.

And Burton? He stayed behind. British geographers found his meticulous scientific notes interesting enough—but that amazing young man, Speke! He had an exciting clue about the Nile.

Speke and Grant did not go to the lake's southern shore. Instead, they arced west around the vast nyanza, through jungles where not even Arab caravans would go. In July, 1862, Speke and the ailing Grant parted; Grant pushed on to the Kingdom of Bunyoro, while Speke led a fast march to the northern shore.

He found it on July 28: a wide river pouring out of Lake Victoria, shattering in a waterfall, rushing away northward. This was certainly the Nile. And his inland sea must be its major source.

In London, Speke's news touched off a sensation. Almost a year later, British crowds jammed his lecture to the point of smashing auditorium windows. The avid public bought all the African adventure books they could find.

Like most sensations, Speke's discovery had bitter opponents. Burton still protested: Guesswork! Speke had not traced the shore, so his "Victoria" might be any number of lakes; he had not followed the river downstream to prove it reached Egypt.

"Poor Speke," the great Dr. Livingstone added politely: He had looked north when he should have looked south. Some of Britain's armchair explorers were less kind, even slanderous.

Fourteen more years of careful exploration followed, and proved how inspired Speke's guesswork had been. The Nile in truth pours out of the nyanza he named for his queen and flows on, through Uganda, the Sudan, and Egypt.

But Speke knew none of this. At the peak of controversy, he died, near Bath, as the result of a hunting accident.

What came after—traders, missionaries, colonists, and finally independence—is the story of mid-Africa as the outside world knows it. It happened incredibly fast. Old Chief Bagaya from the Kingdom of Burundi saw it all in his single long lifetime.

Bustling port of Kigoma lies near the end of an old slave and ivory trade route followed by adventurers who sought the source of the Nile. Passengers waiting for boats to and from points on Lake Tanganyika clog the wharf.

KASIMIA

4

ACROSS THE EQUATOR

WITH A BLAST on the whistle and a gush of green water at the stern, the M. V. *Victoria* puts out from Mwanza near the spot where Speke first gazed over Lake Victoria.

Quiet-voiced Marine Officer James Corbett invited me to his small cabin and told me about the nautical challenges his ship has to meet. "We have a strange problem here—floating islands up to half a mile long," he said. "They're chunks of vegetation that break loose from the shore. If the *Victoria* runs onto one, she can reverse the engines and get off, but less powerful ships have trouble with them."

Thunderstorms crash down with overwhelming force. "In June and July," Corbett told me, "winds get up to gale force and kick up quite a bit of sea." Lake Victoria has plenty of room for squalls—of all the world's inland seas, only the Caspian and Lake Superior are larger.

Westward-bound along the coast of Tanzania, the big white ship passes some permanent islands. Then she swings north. Coffee plantations glide by, and banana groves, steaming after a brief warm rain.

Fuming Nile tumbles into a tortuous rock vise, most dramatic plunge of Murchison Falls' 130-foot descent. Heavy rains that engulfed Uganda in 1961 helped form two lesser falls that thunder as part of Murchison's stairway of cascades.

Farther inland lie the broad open plains where Speke found the Kingdom of Karagwe, semicivilized long before he arrived. He jotted down notes about huge herds of cattle, graceful conical huts 50 feet high, and a hospitable, eccentric king who liked his wives plump and commanded them to sip milk hour after hour, day after day, until they were too fat to stand up.

New passengers clatter up the gangway at Bukoba. A missionary and a tribal chief who is also a cabinet minister, an engineer and a few modern adventurers traveling down the Nile follow their luggage into first-class cabins. Steerage passengers sailing to Uganda scramble aboard, crowding along the deck with bicycles and furniture on their backs.

The ship churns northward again. Barely 25 miles out of Bukoba, Tanzania ends and Uganda begins. The international border runs over the water in an official, invisible line.

Another line, a traceable one, appears on the lake just north of the border. Here a powerful river pours into Victoria, supplying it with more water than any other source except direct rainfall. Maps call this river Kagera. But geographers will recognize it as the main root of the infant Nile. Only a few weeks before, I had followed it in a small plane. Flowing down from Burundi and Rwanda, it meandered like a kinky canal through pasture hills, past dark blots of jungle, and into the swamps of Lake Victoria's shoreland.

Fishermen like this current, a bountiful drift feeding the lake with catfish, elephant-snout fish, lungfish, and sardine-size *Haplochromis.* But even without it, the lake would be a natural protein mine. Here, and in other rich Uganda waters, dugouts and plank canoes skim ashore with 60,000 tons a year.

The prosperity that puts outboard engines on canoes and nylon nets across their thwarts does not end at the shore. Some of Africa's finest soil rolls inland in low, flat-topped hills. Coffee thrives here, and cotton as well. Most of both crops grows on small *shambas,* family farms that colonists were never allowed to take over.

When Speke ventured into these hills, they were part of the powerful Kingdom of Buganda. They still are. Beyond them lie three other royal domains: Ankole, Toro, and Bunyoro.

Then what is Uganda? Four kingdoms and many more tribes complicate the answer, along with customs as far apart as those of Finland and Portugal, and a national radio station that broadcasts in 16 languages. Britain pulled the region together into one big protectorate. With some difficulty, its 7,270,000 inhabitants now strive to fuse themselves into a single people united by hopes as well as by a national boundary.

At daybreak, the *Victoria* glided into Port Bell at the northern end of the lake. British officials spent three months getting to this part of Africa before ships and trains appeared; they walked from the Indian

Last of the primeval giants, elephants in Uganda head for water. Ruthless ivory traders of th

Ocean. Transportation was somewhat better by 1897 when a local king appealed for "ladies to come to teach our ladies"; the English gentlewomen cycled across East Africa. Now, two of our passengers taxied away to an international airport at Entebbe, 30 miles distant. Catching a luncheon flight, they would soar the length of the Nile, over Uganda, the Sudan, and Egypt, arriving at Cairo in plenty of time to dress for dinner.

With nearly two months of land travel ahead of me, I caught a leisurely London-style double-deck bus at the end of the dockyard. A hilly road led us past modern ranch houses, mud huts, small factories—a string of habitation reaching seven miles to the country's capital city.

Kampala—Hill of the Impala—actually has several hills, and the city of 47,000 scatters its buildings at random among green fields and deep green trees. Speke trudged up one of these hills along a fenced avenue through the jungle. On the summit, he found tall thatched buildings of a palisaded town called Rubaga, capital of Mutesa I, King of Buganda.

LIKE the other remarkably advanced kingdoms in this hidden pocket of Africa, Buganda then had a prime minister, a cabinet, a complex system of provincial aristocracy, even a royal brewmaster for the banana beer called *pombe.* With a powerful army and a fleet of huge war canoes, Buganda dominated the region.

But for all its refinement, the kingdom Speke found had its moments of raw savagery. A minor slip in court etiquette, a wave from Mutesa, and drums rumbled over the shrieks of an offender dragged

800's decimated the tuskers. African national parks now protect them from indiscriminate killing.

W. P. KELLER

Women sort coffee at a Uganda plantation. Some 160,000 tons of raw coffee pour from estates each year. The beans dry in the sun, a critical process affecting flavor.

Wading in a sea of leaves, a harvester picks te

Chocolate-brown pods cluster on a cacao tree in a coffee plantation near Kampala. Coffee trees protect the shorter cacao trees from winds. Processed cacao seeds from Uganda help fill the world demand for chocolate and cocoa.

away for execution. When Speke gave Mutesa a carbine, the king ordered a page to find a man in the outer court and shoot him. "And did you do it well?" Mutesa asked when the boy came back.

"Oh yes, capitally," the young page replied; and Speke compared his "look of glee" to the expression of "a boy who had robbed a bird's-nest."

Thirty years after Mutesa died in 1884, the people of Uganda labored up Rubaga Hill with two million bricks to build the twin-towered Catholic cathedral there today. They also built a Protestant cathedral on another summit, and then a dazzling white mosque on Kibuli Hill. Uganda collected the ideas of several worlds as it raced through a dozen centuries in less than one.

It brought its own legacy along, too. Mutesa I is still in Kampala, entombed in a palace of woven reeds. Patrick T. Bakurumpagi, a Buganda Sub-Count with an Oxford accent, took me inside, reminding me to take off my shoes as custom demands.

Mutesa I and two successors lay behind a wall of red bark cloth 40 feet high. Electric lightbulbs dangled from the ceiling, like swollen fireflies in the cool gloom. An old man beat a zebra-hide drum and women chanted, while we sat on the floor mat and the Sub-Count related the history of

NATIONAL GEOGRAPHIC PHOTOGRAPHER JOSEPH J. SCHERSCHEL

n Uganda. Fragrant shrubs, covering about 30,000 acres, produce some 20 million pounds annually.

Buganda's royal family. At that moment, on a nearby hill named Mengo, another Mutesa reigned as heir to 400 years of tradition. A palisade of elephant grass ringed the royal enclosure, where the sacred *gombolola* fire would flicker as long as the ruler lived. In a towered palace lived the king himself—His Highness Edward William Frederick David Walugembe Mutebi Luwangula Mutesa II, thirty-fifth of Buganda's royal line.

But soon after I left Uganda, war drums rumbled from the hills around Kampala. In a clash between Mutesa II and President Milton Obote, government troops burned the royal residence. Scaling palace walls and hailing a taxi, the king escaped. But other crises may follow before Uganda can resolve the conflicts between tribal tradition and modern ways.

The future approaches steadily on yet another Kampala hill. In its classrooms and laboratories, Makerere University College carries on its task of educating enough Washingtons, Jeffersons, and Hamiltons for the country in a single generation.

Back in the valley between the hills, we found a crowded commercial district. I saw farmers in traditional "togas" and Arab *khanzu* robes, coming from their shambas to shop, office girls in prim frocks, housewives elegantly draped to the ankles in six yards of brilliant cotton.

But when Joe Scherschel and I were talking with the taxi driver who took us from hill to hill, he said proudly that he was Goan—his ancestors, civil servants, came from India to work for European administrators.

Dodging fierce traffic on a broad boulevard, we stopped outside a balconied shop and strolled to a cafe. A French mission priest gestured at a sign advertising an American soft drink; an Ismaili Indian from Gujarat delivered it on a tray. Asians in saris, turbans, and European suits crowded the tables around us.

The hedge-wrapped suburbs reminded me of Wimbledon—but with a year-round foam of hibiscus, frangipani, and jacaranda. On the golf course, a Scotsman in white shorts whacked a ball between egrets dotting the fairway. The whole world, it seems, has come to Kampala at one time or another and stayed.

Speke found the Nile at Jinja, 50 miles east. Here Buganda warriors once crossed the river to invade lands of the Basoga tribe. Now a huge smokestack pours white smoke over the city. A foreman showed me around the copper smelter under it.

"We're pleased with our African laborers," he said; "they learn very quickly. Our

"So broad you could not see across it," wrote Speke, who discovered Lake Victoria in 1858. Here it washes upon grounds of a housing project in Entebbe. North, in Kampala, capital and religious center of Uganda, a wedding party (opposite) marches into the Namirembe Cathedral (below).

NATIONAL GEOGRAPHIC PHOTOGRAPHER JOSEPH J. SCHERSCHEL

trouble now is getting enough ore to keep them busy. It comes from the base of the Mountains of the Moon, and rains have been washing out the railway."

Jinja aims to become one of Africa's busiest industrial centers. It gins and spins the local cotton, makes furniture and beer, mills timber and flour. And Jinja planners happily fit the new workmen into blueprints for a city of 40,000. Only Nile-dwellers find the pace a little hard to follow; at dawn, occasionally, disgruntled hippos grunt over an old feeding ground that is now a Jinja street.

A young Under-secretary of State for the Colonies foresaw Lake Victoria as the world's largest reservoir when he visited Uganda. "And what fun," wrote Winston Churchill in 1907, "to make the immemorial Nile begin its journey by diving through a turbine!" He was Prime Minister in 1954 when his vision turned into a swoop of concrete—the Owen Falls Dam—and a power station that sparked new energy from Jinja to Nairobi, 270 miles southeast in Kenya.

So the Nile no longer grates 620 tons of water a second over the rocky rapids Speke found. The falls are submerged now, and the river behaves just as Churchill said it would. It swandives through the dam, then races north for some 100 miles until it bogs down in the lilies and weeds of Lake Kyoga.

John Goddard's party spent four days crossing a 60-mile stretch of the lake. "For hours," he wrote, "we heaved and shoved with our paddles, fighting for every forward boat length through the plant-choked water." Now and then they found an open channel. "Only the phantom whisper of the wind and the occasional haunting cry of an ibis broke the eerie stillness." Free of the lake, the Nile pours west, then veers north to Murchison Falls National Park.

Joe and I reached the park by road from Kampala, setting out in the morning with a laughing Kenyan named Mutua Musyoki as our driver. Black with tar for 33 miles, then red with clay, the road streaks past banana patches and neat little three-acre coffee shambas. Each has a small red-mud hut with thatched roof and a courtyard brushed daily with a bundle of leafy twigs. We dodged bicycles piled high with green bananas, and women, arms laden with bracelets, gliding to market with bundles on their heads.

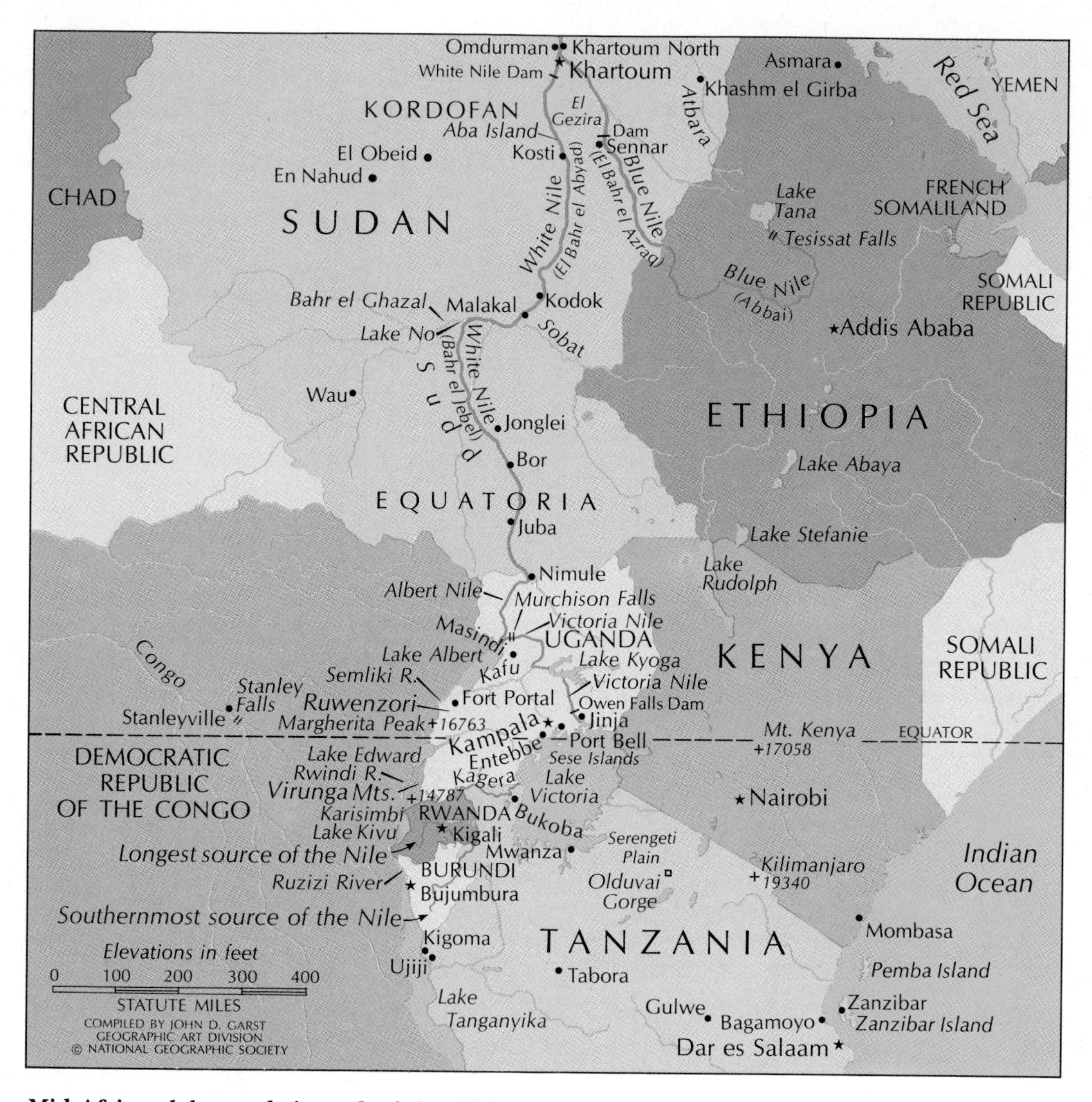

Mid-African lakes and rivers feed the White and Blue Niles on their way to unite at Khartoum.

"Be aware of flying stones," a red-lettered sign warned us. "Many windscreens broken when cars pass," explained Mutua; "throw up stones." Butterflies flurried across the road like colored snowflakes, and birds flitted past—red, gold, electric blue. "Nature makes wonderful birds, doesn't she?" Mutua remarked.

When we crossed the Kafu River, we entered the Kingdom of Bunyoro—drier country, and hotter. As we drove farther north, we saw fewer people. Most of them carried steel-tipped spears, hoping to spot an antelope in the roadside grass.

At Masindi we stopped for lunch and sat listening to the hum of insects and the shouts of Banyoro boys as they kicked a football around with bare feet.

"Park very hot," Mutua predicted as we drove on. "Sweating all the day." When we turned onto the park road, a barrier stopped us at a tsetse-fly control station.

I recalled what a Uganda official had told me: "These flies carry sleeping sickness, you know, that can kill people or cattle. An epidemic killed about 200,000 people from 1906 to 1912, and we moved a million others out of tsetse-fly areas. Man disappeared from that country. Part of it became Murchison Park. So, in a way, we owe the park to that deadly little fly."

Like long-legged birds, workers (opposite) gather salt from Uganda's Lake Katwe, source of some 10,000 tons a year. Sloshing ashore, the villagers balance saline chunks on their heads.

Some 22 miles farther, the hills dropped away, and we drove onto a broad plain of parkland. At once we saw a herd of elephants. I walked within 50 feet of one, and it chased me back to the car at a trot.

We saw animals grazing together, herds of elephants and buffalo, with antelope, warthogs, and guinea fowl.

On a bank high above the Nile, I sat on the terrace of Paraa Safari Lodge and talked with Richard Onslow, Acting Chief Warden, while an elephant ambled by just ten yards away. Hyenas were raiding a garbage bin in plain sight.

"They're quite dangerous," remarked Onslow. "Any animal is dangerous if it's alarmed. We don't encourage tourists to leave their cars. If you're not experienced, you won't see a lion or a rhino until you stumble on it in the high grass. We say, for every animal you see, a dozen see you.

"Don't get out of your car within a hundred yards of an animal," he advised, "and always remember, any creature here can run faster than you can."

"Which ones might attack?" I asked.

"If you run away from an elephant, he'll usually think 'why bother?' and go on his way. A buffalo is more likely to charge. A black rhino will go after you every time, even after a car. If you see one turning toward you, clear out."

I told him that I had walked right up to a herd of hippos dozing in the water.

"We consider the hippo one of our most dangerous animals," he said. "If he takes a bite of something, it's a big bite. They bite cars, you know. They can nip the door off a Land-Rover, glass and everything.

"However," he added reassuringly, "we haven't lost a tourist yet."

For a closer view of the Nile, I took a three-hour launch trip upstream from the lodge. We saw hippos sloshing at the banks, snorting at the gunwales, yawning four feet wide in the wake.

Ahead of the launch, crocodiles lay on sandspits like a log jam. Closer, the high wooded banks slithered as the reptiles slipped into the river. Their legs thrashed wildly for a few moments; then they glided like water-soaked logs, little green eyes shining under warty brows. When the boat had passed, they waddled into the sun again and flopped down, jaws open. Winged

(Continued on page 64)

Resembling waterlogged barrels, hippos loll in the Nile. They wallow in the river all day, emerging nightly like lumbering ghosts to

MARC AND EVELYNE BERNHEIM, RAPHO-GUILLUMETTE (ABOVE) AND EMIL SCHULTHESS, BLACK STAR

forage for grass. Basking beside the Nile, a crocodile (below) cools itself by opening its fearsome jaws. Unperturbed, an Egyptian goose shares the bank with the reptile. Legend says some birds such as the spurwing plover pick bits of food from the teeth of the monsters.

W. ROBERT MOORE, NATIONAL GEOGRAPHIC STAFF

RUSS KINNE, PHOTO RESEARCHERS (ABOVE) AND HELEN AND FRANK SCHREIDER, NATIONAL GEOGRAPHIC STAFF

EMIL SCHULTHESS, BLACK STAR (ABOVE) AND JOHN AND BINI MOSS, PHOTO RESEARCHERS

Colorful array of Uganda birdlife: Tall jabiru, or saddle-billed stork (above), stalks with a deliberate gait through shallow waters of marshes or rivers, then snatches a fish or frog with one lightning thrust of its bill. Master builder, the masked weaver (above, left) enters its tightly knit nest through an underside opening. The sparrow-size craftsman holds down a grass strand with its foot while knotting or weaving the other end with its beak. As many as 300 threads of grass go into the sock-shaped house. A marabou stork (left, center) hunts for mice and lizards. Traders treasure the bright plumage of this ungainly fowl. The whale-headed stork (below, left) seldom leaves marshy areas. The pelicanlike bird, about four feet tall, feeds on turtles, cracking the shells with its thick bill. Golden tiara of wirelike feathers distinguishes the crowned crane (opposite). This stately bird appears on the coat of arms of Uganda.

Like floppy stuffed animals, napping lions drape themselves on branches. The cats lounge on low limbs to escape biting flies and heat.

DAVID GOODNOW

dentists called spurwing plovers hop about inside picking scraps from their teeth, according to local tradition. We came so close to a 14-foot crocodile sleeping on matted swamp reeds that I could have reached out and touched it.

For many years these animals and many others faced extinction. Rich men came to Africa to collect personal museums of the continent's wildlife. Poachers came for ivory. Tribesmen speared game for meats tastier than beef.

Now, the parks protect game so effectively that success means excess. The park has to cull elephants and hippos it cannot support. "Before independence," one official told me, "many people feared the new governments would let their parks deteriorate, but that hasn't happened."

In 1862, the wealthy English explorer Samuel Baker came up the Nile. Braving the whole horrible distance with him was Mrs. Baker, a young and pretty girl, but, as he noted, "not a *screamer.*" They had met Speke and Grant as the two Nile explorers moved north. The Bakers went on southward to discover the greatest watery spectacle on the Nile's 4,145-mile course. They named it Murchison Falls in honor of Sir Roderick Murchison, President of the Royal Geographical Society.

It begins with strings of foam as the river squeezes between narrowing banks. Little whirlpools catch the streaks and swirl them in circles. Standing near the top of the falls, I saw the river raging as it swirled around a bend. Only 20 feet away, water the color of beer boiled a dozen feet above my head.

Then the Nile plunged into a pit at my feet. I leaned over a stone wall to watch the river smashing back on itself like storm waves beating on a cliff. For a moment, the water finds nowhere to go. Then it bursts free, down a gorge shaped like a lightning bolt. It has just dropped 130 feet. Between the wide pool where it recomposes itself and the Mediterranean Sea where it ends, it will descend another 2,000 feet or so.

The pool at the base of the falls is a good place to get bites from hundred-pound Nile perch—or tsetse flies. When the launch turns back, monkeys chatter along the bank, and the air suddenly flutters with birds: yellow masked weaver birds, kingfishers, friendly little wagtails, cormorants that reminded me of Europe's imperial eagles. From their treetop nests, fish eagles survey the Nile.

When night falls, hippos crunch in the grass, unseen. Elephants thump to the banks, huge black shapes in hazy moonlight. Hyenas giggle to themselves, suddenly yelp and bound away. Frogs groan in dark balls of bush on the riverside. Bats swerve at the level of your head. The river slips past like ink full of sequins.

STILL WITHIN THE PARK, the Nile meets Lake Albert and gets a sudden push. Waters of the Great Rift Valley have poured north from Lake Edward and the Semliki River to fill Albert's 1,640 square miles. Baker called this lake the Nile's source when he discovered it. And so it is, in a way. At the northeast tip of Lake Albert, its own water mixes with the Victoria Nile. United, the Nile's major mid-African source waters sweep north as a single river, the Albert Nile, named for Queen Victoria's Prince Consort. For centuries this dank, hot stretch of the river has changed little. Even now, women rustle along the banks dressed in manioc leaves.

Here one of Africa's rarest animals, the white rhino, still survives. International agreement strictly protects it, but poachers hunt it anyway—Asian traders from the coast pay $12 a pound for the horns. These are really lances of hardened hair, ranging from three to ten pounds each. Orientals grind them to powder and sell it as a costly—and ineffectual—aphrodisiac.

About 140 miles from Lake Albert, the placid Nile shatters on a cataract near Nimule. Here, at the Uganda-Sudan border, the river boils with unusual anger. Once the British built a garrison here, and thought their civilization would spread outward from it. But the site was too remote.

"For half a century," Winston Churchill wrote in 1907, "that feeble rushlight of modernity, of cigarettes, of newspapers, of whisky and pickles, had burned on the lonely banks of the White Nile to encourage and beckon the pioneer and settler. None had followed."

Square, massive lip distinguishes this rare white rhinoceros that grazes in the regions of the upper Nile. Murchison Falls National Park in Uganda protects these highly prized animals.

5

AFRICA'S GREAT CHANGE

AFRICA CHANGES in the Sudan. Moving north, the Nile goes from wet country to dry. The word Sudan itself tells of another change, in human terms a far greater one. *Bilad el-Sudan* means "Land of the Blacks," in the language of the Arabs. The Republic of the Sudan gives plenty of room for the transition from Negro country to Arab country. The nation is the largest on the continent: 976,500 square miles, almost five times the size of France.

When the Nile cascades out of Uganda and into the Sudan, it has come nearly a thousand miles and still runs through muggy tropical Africa, with two thousand miles to cover before it reaches Egypt.

This band of water forms a slender physical tie between many of the south's three and a half million people, some Christian but most still pagan, and ten and a half million northerners, largely Moslem. Without the river, the Sudan might never have become one nation. Even with it, unity is under strain.

Signal drums all over the rain-drenched south carry messages of war. Rebellion exploded in 1955 and has smouldered, and flared sporadically, ever since. To quell it, garrisons of the Sudanese army occupy the southern towns. Local tribesmen resent the use of Arabic as the language of education, and resist many Arab ways. Tales of slaughter on both sides have trickled out to the world, and the southern provinces are closed to most travelers.

Beyond Nimule, on the frontier, the river smashes over rocks for many of the next 100 miles. Charles George Gordon, a famous British officer, "prayed" large boats along this stretch in 1875. He finally ordered the rest of his vessels carried in pieces around the rapids.

John Goddard's party portaged their craft too. "Rather than risk our thin-skinned kayaks in the interminable white water," he wrote, "we decided to span this reach on foot...." A government truck carried their gear, while they spent eight days tramping along game trails, "often through 10-foot elephant grass."

Elephants browsed near their camp one night, knocking over trees. The three porters "were not worried; they knew we had a weapon"—Goddard's little .22 rifle. Fortunately, the herd wandered away.

However startled by the white visitors, the villagers accepted them warmly, Goddard reported. "Even when short of food, they... sensed our dependence on them and never let us down."

Less venturesome travelers follow Goddard's northward route on an all-weather

Stork man of the Nile, a Nuer rests by bracing one leg against the other. Little touched by time, thousands of tall tribesmen of Nilotic clans inhabit plains and boglands of the upper Nile provinces of the Sudan.

road that begins in Uganda, passes the rapids, and ends in the Sudanese town of Juba. A car can continue north in the dry season. But the rainy season may last nine months. So most foreigners stroll through Juba to the river and board a steamer bound into the dawn of mankind.

The vessel about to enter one of Africa's most primitive corners is a marvelous contraption. It begins with a flat-bottomed stern-wheeler about 100 feet long, three decks high, and very broad in the beam, drawing no more than four feet of water. When steerage passengers and freight fill the open lower deck, barges are lashed to port and starboard. More barges go at the bow. Furry jets of water gush from the stern, and the whole mobile island pushes slowly downriver.

Chunking past wide and grassy plains, the strange floating community settles in for the eight-day cruise to Kosti, 890 miles north. On the top deck, an Arab captain lights a water pipe and chants steering orders to a turbaned helmsman. First- and second-class passengers are chatting on the screened deck below—government officials, merchants, chiefs.

Third- and fourth-class travelers make a home out of the barges. In one dormitory, men in robes and cloaks—and a few in almost nothing at all—cluster into groups according to their dress. They genially argue politics, or the various fates suitable for a lion that has been killing cattle and children. Cooking smoke wafts overhead, and girls swish laundry in water bucketed from the Nile.

Now and then, the ship splashes between dark forest walls. On the shore, an elephant snorts and hoses its back. Monkeys squeal in the gloom. If a venomous snake

drops onto the deck, a crewman comes with a long stick to prod it overboard.

"The bog," old Africa hands call the mysterious land that begins at Bor, a hundred miles north of Juba. You feel it coming; the air gets heavy, like wet fur on your skin. You see it when the earth seems to melt away in the heat, when black soil becomes mud, then weedy water. Dead ahead sprawls an apple-green horizon—papyrus and grasses, waving 14 feet high in the wind. The paddle wheel sloshes more slowly. The boat eases so silently into the swamp that you can hear a lion roaring far inland.

No one races through the Sudd. One of the greatest swamps in the world—in the wet season, as large as all England—it easily overwhelms the narrow navigation channel. Banks shift, new passages appear. Land that is not quite land oozes and crawls over millions of acres, making a thousand

TOR EIGELAND, BLACK STAR

Provincial policeman wears an Australian-style bush hat on patrol in Juba. About 10,000 men, all volunteers, fill police-force billets in the Sudan. Recruits represent all the ethnic groups of the country, especially Nubians who find the work attractive. Mounted police, though mainly motorized in the Sudan's nine provinces, still ride camels for special assignments.

Sun-bright dresses (above, left) reflect a glint of Western fashion in south Sudan's tribal culture.

Caught in a sudden rainstorm, Juba villagers scurry to shelter. Southern gateway to the Sudan, Juba serves as the administrative capital and commercial center of Equatoria Province, where the rainy season may be nine months long.

Chugging and churning, a Sudanese paddle-wheeler plies the spongy Sudd, a swamp of the Nil

new patterns that will never appear again.

The ship turns into a channel less than 50 yards wide. The helmsman spins the wheel hard right. Hippos blocking the way? Not this time. The starboard barge smashes into spongy shore, groaning with the strain. Birds catapult from the waving reeds like a swarm of insects. "That's how they keep the channel open," an official explains. "They give the bank a good slam every so often."

This strand of the Nile was not always open. When the Emperor Nero sent an expedition to find the river's source about A.D. 66, the Sudd blocked the Romans. Arabs called this place the Barrier—it barred them from new ivory and slave grounds.

In 1880, an Italian adventurer, Romolo Gessi, one of Gordon's officers, was going north through the Sudd by steamer, with an escort of 600 men. Shifting islands trapped them. For three months his men hacked away at the clumps of fetid vegetation, weakened, died of hunger. Some turned to cannibalism. Gessi was one of the few to get out, and he died of the ordeal soon after.

Workers have been chopping away ever since, to clear navigable paths through the Sudd. They never stop. Even today the

TOR EIGELAND, BLACK STAR

nce prehistoric times. Marshy masses drifting in the foreground sometimes choke the channel.

steamer's main deck carries steel chains and huge saws at the bow. If an island blocks the channel, the steamer eases up to it. Crewmen jump ashore. Elegant papyrus tassels wiggle deep in the thicket, as the men rasp apart a vegetable keystone. Then they toss the saws back aboard and tug the chains over the rail, passing them around part of the island. The ship backs off and heaves the blockage out, breaking it into pieces that float downstream.

In the late 1950's a new trap appeared through the Sudd. It looks genial enough —necklaces of pretty blue-purple flowers. But *Eichhornia crassipes*, the water hyacinth, threatens to strangle shipping all over again. The steamers themselves help spread it, since the long weeds tangle in paddle wheels and fall off hundreds of miles away. The government sends weed-spraying teams as far south as Malakal near the swamp's northern rim, but within the Sudd the hyacinth goes wild, beyond control.

Among the tribes of the Sudd, the Shilluk, Dinka, and Nuer are 1,370,000 living reasons for keeping the channel open to northern influences—the only hope of firm national unity. Steamer passengers see why the moment the whistle toots and the ship slips up to a waterside village.

Forty thatched clay-sided houses make a large settlement. Goats bound from doorways as tall, lean tribesmen pop out and run to the shore, holding spears and clubs on their shoulders. Many are fastening burlap-colored cloth around themselves—nudity is now against the law, and the ship may carry soldiers.

Though Arab influence seeps slowly into this land, ancient ways still persist. Wandering ashore, passengers may hear of spirits worshiped and feared today, as in times before the outside world penetrated the region. With luck, they may watch a scarring ceremony, where youths sit calmly to be marked with facial wounds that distinguish the tribe—welts for the Nuer and the Dinka, little raised beads of flesh for the Shilluk, all arranged in patterns.

Long-limbed beauty of the swamp-dwelling Nuer tribe pours beer made of maize through a woven strainer. Wearing only glass beads and ivory bracelets, she—like most Nilotes—considers clothing foolish in the African heat.

OSKAR LUZ

Skin paled by wood ash to ward off mosquitoes, Nuer clansmen rest after a hunt. One sits on a goatskin; ivory bracelets ring his arms. When outdoors, Nuer almost always carry broad spears, their favorite weapon. A tribesman (left) uses straw to thatch his wattle-and-daub hut.

Passengers may see lean herdsmen watching their cattle or waiting to spear a fish. They plant a long throwing spear in the ground and draw one foot up to the opposite knee. Like flamingos, they stand in silence, one-legged and immobile. Some of the tribesmen wear hair as high and firm as crowns. They plaster it with ashes that bleach it to a reddish color.

Sudanese law has explicitly forbidden human sacrifice for some years. A strange law? Not in the Sudd. An old Shilluk tradition held that kings were killed when their health or vigor waned. To the Shilluk, the kingship represents the spirit of the whole tribe. And the tribe believes that when their king, the *reth,* falls ill or grows old, the crops will fail, the cattle will sicken, the people will die—unless they doom the ruling reth.

When the ship's whistle signals departure, mosquitoes are arriving with the night.

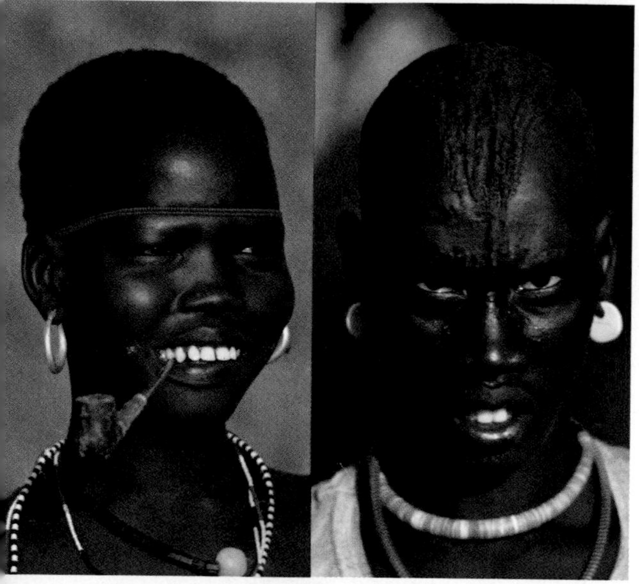

OSKAR LUZ

Descendants of Negroid conquerors, Nuer mirror racial features of ancestors who overran the Sudan some 5,000 years ago. Tribal scars crease the forehead of warrior (right), his hair bleached with ashes. Ivory disks pierce his ears. A maiden (left) wears beads of stone and glass. Like most Nuer women, she smokes a pipe.

Herdsmen move about the village, prodding cattle into special enclosures. Inside these pens, they touch torches to piles of brush or dung—the blue smoke is better for man and beast than the horde of bugs. All along the river, insects hum like distant bagpipes, so thick it seems no air is left to breathe.

The yale, a creature of medieval myth, may have originated in the Sudan. One horn points forward and the other backward, legend said. In later days, the yale wandered into the menagerie of beasts in British heraldry. Today it wanders all around the herdsmen, who have twisted the horns of their precious cattle into many unnatural shapes.

To Sudd tribesmen these big humpbacked animals are life itself; they give milk and, occasionally, blood for food, though only in religious ceremonies are they sacrificed and eaten. A man who wrongs another pays compensation in cattle; a man who wants a wife offers cows as bridewealth, a pledge that he will treat her well.

Cattle belong to the divinity of the clan, and men hold them in almost religious esteem, as the people of ancient Egypt did. In some of the oldest Egyptian tombs, you can see cattle with horns twisted in patterns still favored by the Dinka and the Nuer.

Night brings eerie drama to the Sudd. Walls of papyrus on either side seem to smother the creeping ship in blackness. When the moon rises, it hangs in mist, scattering silver flakes in the wake, painting only faintly an ocean of rustling grass.

Suddenly, the sky ahead may flash red. Around a bend, a swamp fire attacks the channel, spreading wildly across an island. The whole shore is a prehistoric catastrophe, a bastion of snapping flame touched off by lightning, perhaps, or by Sudd-dwellers. With a roar, the wall erupts yellow tongues over the channel and the steamer eases toward the opposite bank.

Frightened by the flames, birds escape through a cloud of ash. The hot blanket spreads north. The Nile there is already a gruel of crocodiles, snakes, rats, waterbuck and reedbuck. Soon the island lies consumed and barren, but within a few weeks it will be as green as ever.

Animals crowd the southern Sudan, and far beyond the river. In 1966, a game department official estimated the number of elephants alone at 50,000. This is still big game country, hard to get to, scarcely touched by foreign safaris.

As a foreign diplomat told me in Khartoum: "Part of old Africa is down there. In some other places," he said with a smile, "if you meet a lion you pat it on the tummy and feed it some potato chips. In the Sudan, you're liable to get eaten."

For some 400 miles the spongy Sudd slides by. Arabs call this part of the Nile *Bahr el Jebel* after its origin—River of the Mountains. Near the end of the swamp, at Lake No, the *Bahr el Ghazal,* River of the Gazelle, slips up from the southwest. The two rivers mix to become *El Bahr el Abyad,* "the White River," the White Nile.

Here it swings east, still staggering through a thousand channels. For years engineers have talked of draining the Sudd, to strengthen the river with water lost through transpiration in plants and evaporation from the heat. They hope to cut

Out on a limb, a Nuer escapes the wrath of a flood that deluged her riverside home. She managed to save gourds used for carrying water.

Haze of smoke from evening fires clouds a Nuer cattle camp. Young range hands drive the

OSKAR LUZ

ɜrd to floodplains when the Nile recedes. Nilotes prize cows as a sign of wealth and prestige.

a canal 200 miles through the spongy land from Jonglei in the south almost to Malakal at the swamp's northern end.

After nearly 80 miles, the river turns northward again. Weak and narrow after its bout with the bog, it carries only 14 percent of all the Nile water that reaches Egypt, but enough to keep the river flowing in dry seasons. The rest of the Nile arrives in tributaries from the Ethiopian plateau to the east. The first of these, the Sobat River, enters here with its seasonal torrent.

THE AIR DRIES, and so does the land. When the ship docks at Malakal, Africa shows signs of change from Negro to Arab. The east bank remains the land of the Dinka, and the Shilluk live just across the river.

But on a tree-dotted avenue as dusty as a traditional Arab main street, passengers find a stone mosque. Men in plump white turbans bicycle past lean Negroes who have come to market in canoes.

Just as one race begins to meet another here, so does ancient meet modern. Among the low, open-sided shops, a merchant may sell frankincense or myrrh, hardware from Khartoum and Germany, canned goods from Egypt and Italy. All the tribesmen in the market wear jewelry, but necklaces of ostrich eggshell and pendants of ivory dangle with strings of factory buttons and, perhaps, a shiny brooch cut from a discarded gasoline can. Yet when the ship churns away from Malakal, it travels for another 300 miles through land held largely by Negro Africans.

Low hills on either side roll like camel humps as the steamer splashes, confidently now, down a broad river. Marshes in the shallows give way to sandy banks. Quite abruptly passengers notice that Africa's great change is completed.

When the ship puts in at Kosti and begins

Scarlet-clad Shilluk amuses his playmates beside the Nile near Malakal. Kings considered divine, as were those of ancient Egypt, rule the Shilluk tribe. Some 100 of their grass-hut communities dot high ground along the Nile.

From a stone counter, a Shilluk fisherman sells his catch at a Malakal market. Until Shilluk introduced net casting, more primitive neighboring tribes fished only with spears.

TOR EIGELAND, BLACK STAR

to swap cargoes for the return trip, men in turbans are hefting bananas and cotton bales. They are dark, certainly, some as brown as the Nuer, but their features are less Negroid. And so much of their past is bound to Islam that they feel themselves unrelated to the people of the south.

In days past, Aba Island, still farther downstream, made a rough dividing point between black Africa and Arab land. More than 28 miles long, once densely wooded, it was the home of Shilluk tribesmen early in the 19th century. But by 1881 it was Arab—a stronghold, in fact, for one of the most electrifying leaders the Arab world has ever seen.

Muhammed Ahmed Ibn el-Sayyid Abdullah rose as suddenly as a sandstorm. Tradition had told of a promised deliverer, one who would come to renew the fidelity of the Moslem to Islam. On Aba Island,

Muhammed Ahmed proclaimed himself that deliverer—the *Mahdi,* he who is guided aright. He was a big, very dark man, known for his holiness. With passionate oratory and a magnetism that fascinated even non-Moslems, he gathered scores of followers. Soon hundreds, then thousands became his *ansaar,* the time-honored name given helpers of the Prophet.

At that time, the Sudan sprawled like an empty ocean—sand, grassland, forest, with neither railways nor roads crossing the country. A few Egyptian garrisons stood like islands in the expanse, controlling it as best they could. Hostility surrounded them. For decades, Egyptian officials sent to rule the Sudan often had been harsh, corrupt—and hated.

The Mahdi proclaimed *jihad*—a holy war. With spears, sticks, and fanaticism, his ansaar became an army. They thundered over Kordofan, the rich central province of the Sudan. They starved out a powerful Egyptian garrison at El Obeid and took its arms and money. Egypt sent an army of 8,000 soldiers, and the ansaar, more than 40,000 strong, butchered them.

An air of fantasy surrounds the Mahdi's storm of success, especially since he was not an easy man to follow. He ordered the ansaar to "abandon all bad and forbidden habits, such as the degrading acts of the flesh, the use of wine and tobacco . . . the clapping of hands, dancing, improper signs with the eyes, tears and lamentations at the bed of the dead, slanderous language, calumny, and the company of strange women."

One who wailed for the dead forfeited his property, a thief lost his right hand on the chopping block. Yet the sweetly smiling leader, then about 40, cast his spell over the whole vast nation. New ansaar streamed to serve him. They would conquer first the Sudan, then Egypt, later Mecca. Finally, Islam would conquer the world.

Evacuate the Sudan, British General Charles George Gordon was ordered when he set out from London in January, 1884. Britain felt responsible for the garrisons there; after all, she had practically assumed control of Egypt. And who would be a better man for the job?

"Chinese" Gordon had already disciplined mutinous forces into an effective army to save the Manchu emperor from rebellion. Later, he had governed all the Sudan for Egypt better than anyone before him. Few doubted that this dashing lone-wolf soldier could get Egyptians out of the country before the Mahdi's ansaar annihilated them.

In Khartoum, Gordon saw the situation differently—how could he evacuate all its 40,000 people? And he could not, in honor, leave any behind.

Nor did he. When Mahdists surrounded the city and cut the telegraph wire to Cairo, Gordon was striding the streets, radiating confidence. Spring went by without full-scale attack, then summer. Clearly the Mahdi meant to starve Khartoum to defeat.

GORDON COUNTED on a British rescue force; by September, it was entering northern Sudan. But it moved slowly, by river steamer and camel. January came, and Khartoum was starving. Everything edible was eaten—donkeys, horses, dogs, rats. People died in the streets by the hundreds, and the living had no energy to bury them. The Mahdists bombarded Khartoum day and night.

The solitary Englishman, his hair turned white with anxiety, promised the rescue force would arrive tomorrow, then the tomorrow after that. Soldiers would get a year's pay for every day they held out. Day after day, Gordon climbed to his palace roof and aimed a telescope across the Nile, looking vainly for steamers.

"I am always frightened . . . ," he wrote in his journal. "It is not the fear of death . . . but I fear defeat, and its consequences."

But no one ever saw him flinch. "Who has said Gordon was ever afraid?" he raged at a merchant who begged him to dim the palace during bombardment. He forced the merchant to dine with him, in front of a window lighted by 24 candles. As they sat like targets, he commanded his guest to go tell all the people in Khartoum "that Gordon fears nothing. . . ."

Riflefire, artillery, and wild shrieking jolted Khartoum awake at three o'clock on the morning of January 26, 1885. The Mahdi's forces were flooding the town,

Shilluk tribesmen lash together the ribs of a new thatched hut. They create the beadlike beauty bumps above their eyebrows by rubbing ashes into a series of small bone-deep incisions.

NATIONAL PORTRAIT GALLERY, LONDON

GEN. HORATIO HERBERT KITCHENER

THE ILLUSTRATED LONDON NEWS

MUHAMMED AHMED IBN EL-SAYYID ABDULLAH

BROWN BROTHERS

GEN. CHARLES GEORGE GORDON

War Commanders: In 1881 Muhammed Ahmed, a religious leader called the Mahdi, proclaimed a holy war to purge Turco-Egyptians from the Sudan. England, aiding Egypt, sent Gen. Gordon to evacuate Egyptians. Islamic fighters seized Khartoum in January, 1885, and killed Gordon. An invasion force under Kitchener smashed the Mahdist rule 13 years later.

hacking down everyone they found, firing houses to drive out more victims. "*es-Saraaya'!*" was one battlecry—"To the palace!" The invaders mobbed the building. According to one report, they found General Gordon on the palace stairs, in a white uniform, "standing with a calm and dignified manner, his left hand resting on the hilt of his sword." They speared him to death.

The British rescue force came two days too late. It retreated down the Nile.

Five months later, the Mahdi died. But under a fierce, charming Khalifa named Abdullah, his movement endured, ruling an empire half the size of Europe.

Not for 11 years did Britain move again. Public indignation demanded a massive campaign to end the Mahdist threat. For a leader, the British Government chose Gen. Horatio Herbert Kitchener, a tall, steel-cool officer with a solid career behind him at the age of 46.

The army requisitioned Nile tourist steamers from Thomas Cook & Son. It massed 11,000 soldiers on the Sudan's northern border. For more than two years troops advanced up the Nile, swelling the force to 25,000, bringing artillery and gunboats, bagpipes, flutes, and brass bands.

On September 1, 1898, Kitchener drew up his army on a dry, sandy plain outside the Mahdist capital city, Omdurman. At dawn the next day, 52,000 ansaar screamed down on his British and Egyptian troops.

"It was not a battle," reported a correspondent, "but an execution." The ansaar, badly armed, charged straight into a holocaust of artillery.

"At half-past eleven," the young cavalry officer Winston Churchill later wrote, "Sir H. Kitchener shut up his glasses . . . remarking that he thought the enemy had been given 'a good dusting'. . . ."

Only 40 years after Speke looked over Lake Victoria for the first time, the Nile was an open river. From its remote sources deep in the land of the blacks to the Arab shore of the Mediterranean, it was ruled by the imperial powers of Europe.

Bursting shell from a British gunboat showers debris on Moslem warriors in this contemporary sketch of river fighting during a 317-day struggle for Khartoum in 1884. British river bombardment of villages near the city failed to break the siege that brought victory to the Mahdi.

6

TWO RIVERS TO KHARTOUM

TWO NILES MEET at Khartoum. The White Nile has come north in a gentle arc from Aba Island, where tenants work a 30,000-acre farm owned by descendants of the Mahdi. Splitting around more islands on the western edge of Khartoum, the waters are 2,265 miles from their southernmost source, and still 1,880 miles from the Mediterranean Sea.

The second river, flowing along the northern edge of Khartoum, looks on the map like just another tributary, another root of the whole Nile tree. But *El Bahr el Azraq* —the Blue Nile—is far more than that. In volume it ranks as the greatest river of the system. The Blue Nile provides 58 percent of all the water carried across the desert to Egypt in the course of a year.

A major river in its own right, it stretches 1,007 miles, as closely as geographers can measure it, beginning high in the wild mountains of Ethiopia. By jet I flew to the region of its main source, a strange, silent lake named Tana that spread below like a huge blue valentine. Sun splashed the earth like liquid heat, nourishing luxuriant verdure. Yet by nightfall, I knew, the air would turn quite cold, for Lake Tana lies more than a mile above the level of the oceans.

Like a narrow ribbon, the Blue Nile winds through Ethiopian highlands. Summer rains swell this 1,000-mile-long artery that joins the White Nile at Khartoum, bringing tons of silt to enrich fields of the Sudan and Egypt.

A Portuguese priest, Father Pedro Paez, was apparently the first European to see it. After years as a prisoner of Arabs, he made his way into Ethiopia in 1603 and stayed to evangelize. His teachings were not entirely new to the country. Missionaries from Egypt had brought Christianity to the Semitic kingdom in the fourth century. The religion remained strong among scattered Ethiopian peoples.

Like many of the Christians in Egypt, they rejected the doctrine of Christ's two natures, human and divine, that the Council of Chalcedon defined in 451. Westerners came to call their faith "Coptic"—a name referring to the people descended from ancient Egyptians, and distinguishing the church of Egypt from other groups in the world of Christianity.

Though Father Paez won few converts, the Emperor Susenyos accepted his teachings in 1621, and the priest built a large Roman Catholic church at the northern end of Lake Tana.

Father Paez would recognize Lake Tana at once. Fishermen paddle rafts of papyrus stem over the 1,200-square-mile surface. All along the shores, Coptic churches, round and thatched, stand as they did long before his house of worship rose.

On the southern shore, monkeys chatter as an antelope tiptoes out of the forest to drink. Low islands stand on the water like little baskets of trees, and occasionally a python four times as long as a man writhes from one island to the next.

The Blue Nile slides out to a series of rapids at the tip of the heart-shaped lake. Some day a dam here may control its flow, giving more electricity to Ethiopia. But today the river flows unimpeded, going wild a few miles downstream.

Tesissat—Big Smoke—Falls is the deepest plunge, a crescent where the river splits and tumbles in 150-foot plumes. Around the falls and throughout the region, birds by thousands build their nests. Beyond the roar of the waters rings a musicbox of sound from metallic-blue starlings, black and white kingfishers, storks, ibis, and giant hornbills with snow-tipped wings.

When morning moisture fumes around ferns and palms and acacia trees on the banks, you can follow the curve of the river in a streak of cloud that hangs hundreds of feet over its gorge. But following it in any other way is hazardous. Rapids and

Buoyant papyrus raft, like those of ancient Egypt, skims Lake Tana, source of the Blue Nile

"Its scales a sheen of spotted gold," wrote Virgil of the African python. Called a rock python, the reptile *(Python sebae)* ranges savannas and forests as well as stony lairs south of the Sahara. This constrictor can exceed a length of 30 feet, preys on wild game, and will attack man. Many African tribes once worshiped the python, often punishing anyone who harmed it.

his reed-woven craft, called a *tanqua,* quickly becomes waterlogged and must be dried often.

NATIONAL GEOGRAPHIC PHOTOGRAPHER JAMES P. BLAIR (BELOW) AND NORMAN R. LIGHTFOOT, PHOTO RESEARCHERS

cataracts menace the toughest boats. And I learned that Blue Nile tribesmen attacked and killed explorers as recently as 1962.

So, mostly in solitude, the river slices like a carving knife through the saw-toothed plateau of Ethiopia. In places the gorge is 4,000 feet deep—dank, eerie, malarial, the home of crocodiles and hippopotamuses, where even local people are afraid to go. Often it narrows until dark cliffs shut out the sun. Elsewhere the walls spread 15 miles apart, leaving space for villages and mighty tributaries that enter as fans of thick gray silt.

Not until 1960 was this mysterious gorge fully mapped. United States Government technicians worked with Ethiopian colleagues for four years to study the region's rainfall and soils, to measure elevations and water flow. They traveled by truck where they could, then by mule. Often they used helicopters, flying in a single day to places an explorer of the 1920's and '30's trekked for months to reach.

More than 500 miles from Lake Tana, the mountains dissolve. The Blue Nile calms, and flows onto the flat plains of the Sudan. But even here it remains capricious. Low and languid in spring, it becomes a torrent during Ethiopia's summer rains. At its peak, the river may rush along with more than 3,500 times the volume of water it carries at its weakest stage, according to hydrographs at the Sudan border.

Men have been recording the annual Nile flood ever since 3100 B.C. For just as long, they have been trying to trap it, first with canals and embankments, then with controlled-level dams called barrages, more recently with mountains of stone and earth and concrete.

Present plans envision more than 20 dams corking up the Blue and the White Nile from end to end. Some of these dams already stand. Half of the total control system might be operating by 1975.

What does a dam do to the desert? When I asked Sudanese, they answered with floods of details. Water is so precious in some parts of their country that men shovel 250 feet downward to find it. Elsewhere, they dig a moat around a baobab tree, wait for the rains, then bucket as much as 1,000 gallons into the hollow trunk for storage.

In these regions, when water comes it nurtures nothing less than a miracle.

GEORG GERSTER

Hat-shaped mounds of cotton lie on a field in the Gezira, a clay plain between the Blue and White Niles in central Sudan. A small earth bank around the edge of the cleared area, called a harvest square, protects the piles of cotton against irrigation flooding. In 1925 officials launched the Gezira Scheme, channeling Nile water that now irrigates 1.9 million acres. The project created a livelihood for thousands of tenant farmers by changing wasteland into the Sudan's richest area of cotton production. Teasing out ginned cotton in a humid room, Sudanese laborers (left) resemble ballet dancers as they juggle soft masses of the cash crop. This process adds moisture, making the long fibers less brittle and easier to bale. Bundles of white gold (below) await railway passage to Red Sea ports. Gezira cotton reaches world markets and provides more than half of the Sudan's export income.

TOR EIGELAND, BLACK STAR (ABOVE) AND BRUCE BRANDER, NATIONAL GEOGRAPHIC STAFF

Canopy of lebbek leaves shades En Nil Avenue in Khartoum, capital of the Sudan. From the shoreline avenue (below, left) the Blue Nile Bridge stretches to Khartoum North. The Blue Nile splits and flows around Tuti Island (center), streaming into the White Nile (upper left) between Tuti and Omdurman in the background. In 1885, a Moslem uprising of ansaar overwhelmed a fort manned by troops under British command on Tuti Island.

I found just such a miracle in the Gezira area, along the Blue Nile. In 1925, a stone masonry dam almost two miles wide began its work near the dusty, viciously hot town of Sennar. Through a network of canals water streamed into a huge, arid triangle of land between the two Niles.

Now the Gezira project and its extensions cover nearly 1,900,000 acres, a highly organized tenant farm. Here many thousands of Sudanese families rotate their food, fodder, and cotton crops according to plan, and share profits with the government. Where nomads once hauled drinking water from 120-foot wells, the Sudan has found a treasure house. Cotton grown here, with its extra-long fibers, is some of the finest in the world, and annually it brings in more than half of the nation's earnings from abroad.

Though luxuriant land is new to the Blue Nile desert, wealth and importance have been here before. About the time that Spain's *conquistadores* landed in the New World, a horde of Negro warriors appeared along this part of the river and set up their capital at Sennar. No one knows where they came from. But soon much of the world was hearing of the dynamic kingdom they established—the Fung Empire, reaching from the Red Sea westward beyond the White Nile, stretching north almost to the border of Egypt.

From Sennar, a veiled monarch in golden robes sent armies in steel mail and copper helmets to conquer lesser kings, bringing rich tribute to the Blue Nile city. His merchants cast trade routes as far as India.

But between 1700 and the start of the next century, the great empire decayed. In 1821, the last of the Black Sultanate, a small, bewildered man named Badi VI, gave up his crumbling capital to an invading army from Turkish Egypt.

The conquerors made their headquarters in a fishing village where the Blue and the White Nile come together. *El Khartoum*—elephant's trunk—the area was called. The shape of the confluence suggests the animal's head, with the Blue Nile as the trunk. Khartoum grew into a squalid place, where thousands of people crowded into mud huts and left dead animals to rot in the streets. The victorious Mahdists demolished it almost completely in 1886, using Omdurman, just across the main Nile, as their capital.

Victorious in turn, General Kitchener became governor-general of the Sudan, and ordered Gordon's ruined palace restored, filled with marble, great mirrors, and fine furnishings.

As the 19th century passed away, 5,000 workmen rebuilt the entire city of Khartoum in the shape of a Union Jack. Imperial arrogance? Perhaps. But sound strategy: machine guns could dominate the streets with ease if the Sudan exploded again. The explosion never came.

British rule was orderly and incorruptible; the Sudan, weary of wars and plunder, accepted it. For nearly six decades the country was under a condominium. Technically, Egypt and Britain governed it jointly. Actually, a small group of impeccably trained British officials watched over the vast nation. From all evidence, they did their job well. Foreign settlers never took over Sudanese land, even where tropical

plantations might have flourished. Independence came with relative ease in 1956. And today people recall the British with little resentment, and much respect.

Modern Khartoum offers a desert surprise. For hundreds of miles around, the land stretches out, hard and arid. Often mirages blot the tan plains with fantasy lakes. In summer, dust storms called haboobs can turn the whole atmosphere into a red fog. Yet I found the capital city green from the Blue Nile to the White, and I remembered Kitchener gratefully—he had ordered 7,000 trees planted along the avenues so the people could enjoy cool grottoes of shade.

From my hotel on En Nil Avenue, I strolled under heavy branches along the Blue Nile shore. Block after block, past and present flow together smoothly. Kitchener's old gunboat *Melik* bobs as shipshape as ever, moored at a muddy bank. I inspected the armor plated wheelhouse, with its machine guns dated 1893 still in place. Today members of the international Blue Nile Sailing Club meet there on the main deck.

To find the place where Kitchener lived, I had to ask for "Republican Palace," but its guards still wear the starchy white uniforms of empire days. In the cooler hours, after sunset, I hailed one of the little yellow taxis whizzing along by the dozen, and rode past wooden waterwheels creaking up gallon after gallon of the Nile.

On a terrace at the old Grand Hotel, turbaned merchants flap out carpets and arrange displays of ostrich feathers, carved ivory, reptile skins, and lion-fur sandals. With a little graceful bargaining, I bought ivory letter-openers shaped like crocodiles.

Next door, in the air-conditioned Sudan Hotel, modern merchants bargain too, over a shipment of waterpumps for the backlands, perhaps, or machinery for the industrial suburb of Khartoum North.

Down the street, a sizable zoo displays the animals of the Sudan. But not far away, in flood time, a city dweller might shoo a ten-foot crocodile out of his garden.

KHARTOUM has always been an international city. Greeks and Britons make their homes here, among Syrians, Egyptians, and Italians. Differences often melt together. A Hungarian restaurateur regularly serves Neapolitan spaghetti to turbaned diners. And on Sunday, 48 hours after Islam's day of rest and worship, a congregation gathers in the Cathedral of All Saints to chant Anglican prayers in the Arabic accents of the Sudan.

Omdurman spreads along the Nile's west bank, a city in a different world altogether. On its dusty, treeless shore, the Mahdi's ansaar began with a small mud village and ended up with a community six miles long. The present city of 171,000 is, after Cairo, the largest city on the Nile.

TOR EIGELAND, BLACK STAR

Sensitive fingers shape an ebony figurine. Its smooth, quiet surface reflects Sudanic art style. Except for Egyptian art forms, earliest African sculpture dates from the Nok culture that thrived in the Sudan region south of the Sahara about 200 B.C.

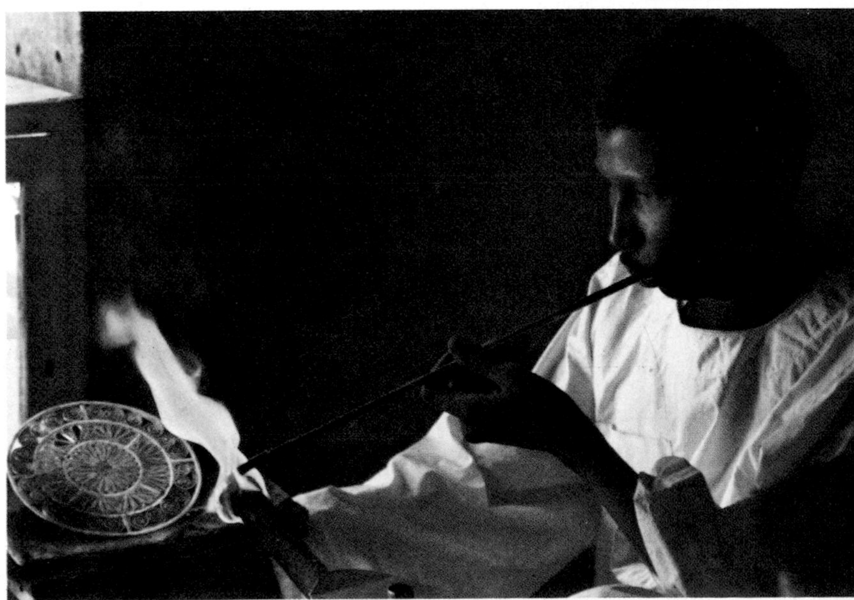

Skilled silversmith softens and molds a filigree service tray. He directs flames by blowing through a tube. Today in the Sudan artisans trained to use machines gradually replace the remaining handcraftsmen who work with ivory, wood, leather, and silver.

Wholly Arabic in character, Omdurman is a city of the desert. I wandered one morning along its hot streets paved only with the red dust that swirls up in the haboobs. Goats, robed people, and donkey traffic flow between low walls of compacted mud. In each wall, a dozen cracked doors hang open on cast-iron hinges. Inside is a courtyard and a little tan house, a box of shade in a dazzling world where 100° F. in midwinter surprises no one.

These buildings, made of unfired brick, tend to dissolve with time and six inches of annual rainfall, so few of them survive from the Mahdi's day. Yet a good guide knows where to find part of the old slave market. I could still peek through the gunports in a fortress wall of mud and straw, for a view over the Nile. Not far away, I could see the Mahdi's tomb, destroyed by the British, now restored. Above its silver-painted dome an emblem shines in the sun: the spear of the Sudan and the crescent of Islam, visible for miles.

Gliding like white shadows, draped women stroll in Omdurman. One gown, or *tob,* unfurls a colorful embroidered hem. A single sheetlike piece of cloth worn over a shift or dress, the tob varies in quality, ranging from unbleached muslin to fabric woven with gold thread. Some Sudanese women drape themselves in luxurious silk tobs imported from Switzerland.

Bathtub for camels, trucks, cars, and donkeys, the Nile since Biblical days has furnished washing water. Today, besides cleaning clothes and animals in the river, Omdurman residents scrub their vehicles in the shallows.

Smug dromedary strikes a pose as if to attract a buyer at the camel market in Omdurman. Bargaining camel breeders huddle with a trader; he will buy the animals for export to Egypt. Omdurman and El Obeid in central Sudan rank as the country's major livestock trading centers. In Omdurman the market opens about midday three times a week; desert nomads offer camels that sell for an average price of $70.

TOR EIGELAND, BLACK STAR

TOR EIGELAND, BLACK STAR

With more luck than mine, one might see the Mahdists themselves on the march. General Kitchener was not counting on Arab resilience when he wrote in 1899: "Mahdism is now a thing of the past. . . ."

Today, when crisis threatens the government, ansaar by the thousand may close in on Omdurman and Khartoum. A buffalo horn bellows advance. In double column, the army shuffles forward thundering the battle chant: *"Laa ilaaha illa llaah, Muhammadun rasuulu llaah"*—"There is no God but Allah, and Mohammed is his prophet."

Wise and diplomatic descendants of the first Mahdi long ago dropped the fiercer aspects of the movement. They encouraged its followers to study European languages and literature, science and government. Not only did Mahdism survive, it remains today the strongest traditional force in the Sudan. A foreign embassy official in Khartoum told me: "The Mahdists threatened to call about 30,000 men to demonstrate here during a recent bit of trouble. Nobody doubted that they could do it."

And the sect's political leader, El Sadik El Siddik Abdel Rahman El Mahdi, took time to tell me more. As the new nation struggles to organize its vast territory, he stays excessively busy. But when I visited his Omdurman villa, a few blocks from the Nile, he received me with leisurely hospitality, as if nothing could be more important than the questions of a guest.

"Was the first Mahdi your direct ancestor?" I asked.

"He was my grandfather's father," the tall, bearded Sadik replied. Ceiling fans were swishing away the heat, and white-robed ansaar glided into the reception room to serve vanilla-flavored milk.

I risked a more delicate question: "Why do some historians describe him as a villain and call him 'the Mad Mahdi'?"

"Perhaps because they took most of their information from British military records," he answered politely. His quick command

Influential brothers: Sayed Ahmed El Mahdi (left), owns sprawling quarters (above) in Khartoum. Nephew of the present Mahdi, he meets with religious leader Imam El Haadi El Mahdi (center), and Sayed Yahia El Mahdi, head of Dhairat El Mahdi, a family business organization that includes a large cotton-growing and ginning enterprise and a construction company.

BRUCE BRANDER, NATIONAL GEOGRAPHIC STAFF

Spokesman for millions, El Sadik El Siddik Abdel Rahman El Mahdi became the Prime Minister of the Sudan in July, 1966. Called Mahdi, a Moslem messiah, he also commands a strong following of ansaar, ardent warriors ready to die for the holy cause of Mahdism.

brought servants back into the room with a set of books on the Sudan that the 30-year-old Sadik had written. Moments later, small cups of thick sweet coffee clinked onto the ivory-inlaid table before us, and the Oxford-educated leader explained more about modern Mahdism.

With independence came a need for many basic policies, both internal and international. Some stir deep concern, as in the days of Queen Victoria. Demonstrations have been aimed against union with Egypt, and against communism.

Nor does Sadik, strongest voice in the powerful Umma Party, favor copying political plans from the West, even though he leans in that direction.

Instead, he exerts his influence—recently augmented as he became the Sudan's new Prime Minister—to keep the country within its own traditions, interpreting them to include city-dwellers and nomads, primitive farmers and modern manufacturers in Africa's largest nation.

TOR EIGELAND, BLACK STAR

Stronghold of Mahdism: Aba Island, original seat of the Mahdist movement, greets a throng of ansaar, world's largest private army and backbone of this Islamic sect in the Sudan. The warriors wear a white turban distinguished by a small tail in the back. Forbidden firearms, they carry spears, swords, and the Mahdi's flag emblazoned with crossed spears and crescent moon (center and opposite). In 1883 Aba Island served as headquarters of the first Mahdi when his spearhead of warriors drove Turco-Egyptian troops from the country. Today the ansaar exert political force rather than military might. "They feel it is their duty and mission to sacrifice everything for the glory of the Sudan," said one Mahdist leader.

Bell-shaped dome of the first Mahdi's tomb towers above a wedding reception in Omdurman.

TOR EIGELAND, BLACK STAR

The Imam of the Mahdist movement often marries many couples at once in ceremonies here.

7

NORTHWARD THROUGH NUBIA

THE WHITE NILE runs green, some say, and the Blue Nile flows brown. The White looks blue, protest others, and the Blue is red. Then again, the White might run gray and the Blue true-blue. So the argument goes, a popular controversy among Nile travelers for a half-century.

Actually, the rivers change colors. The White Nile often flows green, though I found it tinted gray with silt. The Blue Nile alters even more dramatically. For much of the year, water the color of emeralds slips past Khartoum. But from June to October, a gruel of rain and tons of mud gushes down from Ethiopia, turning the river the color of rust. Then, as the Blue Nile meets the White, they continue their journey side by side in one channel, refusing to mix for miles.

The southern border of Nubia is somewhat less definite than the colors of the rivers. With no political status of its own, the ancient land of the Nubian people lacks precise boundaries. Some say the Nile enters Nubia around Khartoum. But linguists offer more exact limits. Their Nubia starts 350 river-miles north, where people ranging in color from fair to very dark speak dialects of the Nubian language. In any case, the Nile flows northward through Nubia until it reaches Aswân in Egypt.

Jeweled women of Nubia wear festive finery. Their forebears lived on the Nubian Nile centuries before the rise of ancient Egypt. Reluctantly, some 100,000 Nubians vacated homesites as the Aswân High Dam backed the Nile into Lake Nasser and flooded their land.

Travelers can go the same way by air or rail. By river, the trip to Egypt is difficult, since the Nile stutters over a succession of rapids on its way to the border and even small-boat navigation halts at many of them.

By road, with a good desert guide, a tough vehicle, and something soft to sit on, you can set out from Khartoum with a fair chance of reaching Egypt in a few days.

I hired a driver who knew the area, and a small truck. For the first dozen miles, a paved road seemed encouraging. Even when it dropped off its own shoulder and became a track on lumpy soil, the fresh tireprints of a road-grader made me wonder why no one else was taking this route.

The first *wadi* explained in shuddering detail. The truck rocketed into the dry riverbed and slammed to earth. Spare springs crashed behind the driver. We bounced from seat to ceiling.

The wheels ignored the shock and spun on at 20 miles an hour while yellow sand flowed around them like honey. After the sand came mud ruts that rocked the whole machine like a boat.

If a rainstorm breaks, a Scottish engineer had warned me, a wadi only a few yards wide can be lethal. Rain slides quickly off the hard desert. It runs into tiny wadis that lead, like twigs on an oak tree, to larger branches. A brief shower can surge down a main trunk in something resembling a tidal bore. Unwary drivers have lost their trucks, and nearly their lives, within 30 miles of Khartoum.

Often, though, the driver can see a wadi before he hits it, when low trees mark the banks like pale green marching columns. Yet even a canny desert hand can fail to spot the orderly verdure in a confusion of acacia trees that shade the plain like thousands of beach umbrellas.

This region of semidesert, running in a wavy stripe across the entire continent, nourishes a surprising amount of life with only four to fourteen inches of rain a year. Bright yellow-green birds flash about like feathered darts. Goats nuzzle a fuzz of tan grass, and dance on hind legs under the trees to nip at lower leaves. Camels, in sleepy composure, chew upper branches. Their owners doze in the circle of shade below after a lunch of white goat cheese, round bread loaves, and a brown, crumbly sweet made of sesame seed and honey.

Both herds and people spend the winter here on the edge of starvation. In spring, they travel south to meet the rains, and then follow them back again. The rains cease at about 18 degrees north latitude.

About 50 miles out of Khartoum, our truck whined between huge natural rock piles. Within an hour's hike from us, the Nile squeezed through a chasm walled in granite, eight miles long. This is the first of the six cataracts that blocked ancient travel—the first, counting from the south. But officially it comes last, since we still number them as the ancient Egyptians did—the First Cataract at Aswân and the Sixth Cataract here.

None of them plunge in a spectacular waterfall, as the name "cataract" suggests. Usually, the river splits and staggers over ribs of dark, water-polished rock that cut across its bed. Then it recomposes itself, often moving into deep rock gorges. Goddard's party found the Sixth "mild"—"a cataract for beginners."

Beyond it, he wrote, "we enjoyed some of the loveliest landscapes of the Nile. Fertile green banks climbed to groves of date palms and irrigated gardens. White sand beaches fringed granite islets covered with luxuriant grass and shrubs."

This broken line of green continues all the way to Egypt. Often it narrows to a few feet; sometimes it spreads two and a half miles into the beige desert.

"Cast thy bread upon the waters:" the Bible exhorts, "for thou shalt find it after many days." From Khartoum to the Mediterranean, Nile farmers did just that for thousands of years. The annual flood, never failing, filled the cracked earth and left a fresh film of silt. With the fertile new soil as moist and sticky as library paste, sometimes even before the water had drained away, farmers drilled holes with sticks and tucked seeds into them.

Some of the land above flood level still gets water from the *shadoof* or the *sakieh*—both simple machines, both used for centuries—but diesel pumps are gradually taking over. Already the engines bring water

BRUCE BRANDER, NATIONAL GEOGRAPHIC STAFF (BELOW) AND GEORG GERSTER

Digging with a *seluka* stick, a *fellah*—Arabic for farm worker—jabs seed holes in Nile mud. Such riverside gardens, rich with silt deposited by the river, yield maize, millet, and barley.

Across a golden crest of sand, a Nubian goatherd strings her flock. Since the Stone Age, when lush pastures waved where desolate sand now blows, Nubians have tended goats and sheep.

to half of the Sudan's irrigated area, and they spout along the river throughout Egypt as well.

Villages stand back from the Nile on useless land, rows of little tan and whitewashed houses. More than 600,000 Sudanese live in them. In the 1,000 river miles between Khartoum and the Egyptian border, these people harvest their livelihood from only 500 square miles of fields.

Citrus trees and date palms flourish here, and recently a processing plant opened at Karima, near the start of the Nubian language country. This factory now packages fruit for export and conducts experiments with date alcohol, date liqueurs, and blends of date and citrus juices. It has plenty of raw material; more than 30,000 tons of dates mature every year within walking distance of the Sudan's northern Nile.

ROAD TRAVELERS see little of this. The river usually lies out of sight. Sometimes I thought I saw it, but an ocean of heat waves made it indistinguishable from one of the shiny blue mirages.

Often I could not distinguish the road either. At times the driver had to choose his way from a maze of tire streaks meandering over the broad, glaring flats. And once we nearly got lost in a sparse maze of acacia trees, until we spotted in the vague distance a cargo truck pulling a pennant of dust along the regular trail.

Camels used to sway along this trade route. They still converge on it from the backlands, bringing baled animal skins and gum arabic—balls of acacia sap—to the local railheads. But trucks are gradually taking their business away, carrying goods at one-third to one-seventh the current cost of camel freight.

On train day, you find both trucks and little caravans where the road meets a lonely stripe of rails. The vehicles stand on squares of black shade, hoods open to let the engines cool. Camels doze and drool and growl on their knees around a station house of mud brick.

Tiny communities cluster around each station: huts with conical sun hats of yellow thatch, some tents puffing up like tan bubbles, a few tall tombs that reminded me of inverted wine goblets. Yet the place seems abandoned, its people tending their flocks far over the desert, and cargo drivers

In nuptial garb, a bridegroom in the village of Tûshka sits outside his house to accept donations for wedding expenses. He or his family will repay the money piled beneath his Koran—more than $500—as the contributors themselves marry. Before resettlement offered greater opportunities, most young Nubian men left home to seek work, often in Cairo or Khartoum. As a rule only the elderly, the children, and the women inhabited the villages. The men returned to marry. Lacking land or employment they departed again to earn wages to support their families.

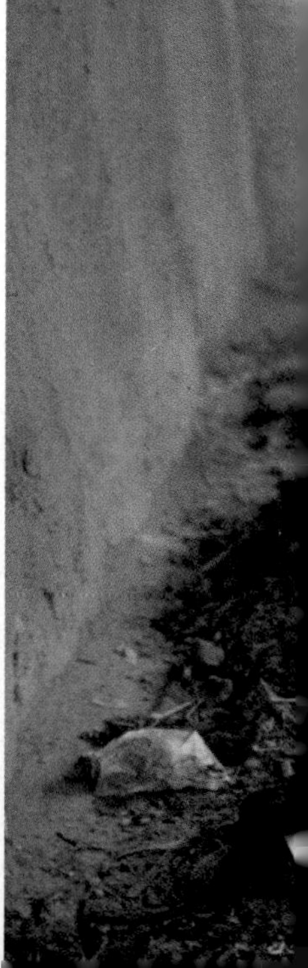

GEORG GERSTER

Gift for the bride, shoes arrive in the classic style, balanced on the bearer's head. Second woman brings a similar gift for the mother of the bride.

Makeshift bakery in Tûshka gleams with straw fires and flashing smiles. Women prepare wafer-thin disks of bread for 500 wedding guests from far up and down the Nile. They lift the unleavened cakes from hot griddles with sticks, then turn them with the hands.

hiding from the sun inside black doorways until the train wails into hearing.

Shendi was a desert treasure house 150 years ago. The town produced almost nothing. But it lay in the path of three great caravan trails. Its king held a hoard of personal wealth and absolute power, with 300 horsemen available to him and 20 firelock rifles.

Camel trains jingled in from Egypt and central Sudan, from Ethiopia and Red Sea ports. Slaves, gold, horses, Venetian beads, German swords—Shendi's famous *suq*, or market, had them all. Invaders from Turkish-ruled Egypt devastated the town in the 1820's, but it gradually revived as a trading center.

Now the provincial capital, Ed Damer, handles more goods than Shendi, but on Mondays and Thursdays—market days—Shendi's suq remains very busy indeed.

When your truck bogs down in market crowds, you might just as well get out and walk. Along either side of the broad dusty avenues, mud-brick arcades hold a hundred little shops. Nomads in ragged robes wander past, swinging shiny aluminum cooking pots. Women in black and pink and sky-blue cotton billow from stall to stall with bundles on their heads. Merchants

GEORG GERSTER

Stained and streaked by the river, temples of Philae Island rise from Nile mud. For years waters impounded by the old Aswân Dam climbed up the pylon of the temple of Isis (right) and submerged the colonnades of the unfinished kiosk (left). Today dikes box in Philae to keep it dry in the waters between the old and new Aswân Dams. Ptolemaic Greeks and Romans built the monuments. As late as the sixth Christian century ailing pilgrims converged on the temples, believing they had healing powers.

sit cross-legged behind stacks of fruit and firewood, behind baskets of beans and piles of grain freshly winnowed onto reed mats. Men haggle pleasurably over sheep and goats. A few camels wait sleepily at a hitching post to be sold. Not too long ago a good one cost $50; now you would pay an average price of $70.

The truck waits outside a plastered building on the main square. Travelers automatically stop here, as I did, to pay a courtesy call on the local government inspector. He looks stern as he strides from a flowery courtyard, a dark, muscular man in khaki shorts. Closer, he smiles widely and leads his visitors out of the 120-degree sun. Coffee? Mint tea? Or cola? The guide whispers an explanation of Arab hospitality: "You can choose but not refuse." In a half-hour visit, I ended up with all three.

Beyond Shendi, the land turns starkly barren. Acacia umbrellas vanish altogether for miles at a time. Tiny walled villages cling to hilltops like desert forts, but no life moves around them. Then, at sunset, a few enshrouded women glide outside the walls of mud or acacia branches, peer over the gilded country, and vanish to cook the evening meal. Herdsmen stride home with the giant steps of the plains-dweller, each clutching a long stick to guard against wild dogs.

Faraway headlights wink as cargo continues to move in the cool of night. To keep to the trail, the driver may follow a set of tail-lights that flare in a plume of dust as if the truck carrying them was on fire. Or he may navigate by the stars. Looking up, I found all the jewelry of heaven glistening in the dry, clear air, a pale sheet of light with the Southern Cross and a few other brilliant constellations shining out like tiny beacons.

About 140 miles out of Khartoum, less than an hour past the village of Kabushiya, the Nile slides by the first major trace of ancient civilization along its northward course. At night, I almost mistook the ruined palaces of Meroë, a quarter-mile from the river, for a natural dip in the ground. But at sunrise the depression takes on a clear rectangular shape. Broken walls enclose it. In the rubble where the palaces stood, goats graze around pillar stumps and curly-coated rams of stone.

Egypt did not extend this far into the land of Kush, as the northern Sudan was known during the days of the Pharaohs. But its influence did. Waves of plunderers, traders, and conquerors cascaded up the Nile from 3000 B.C. onward. Snefru, who ruled Egypt before the Great Pyramid was built, left an early and detailed record of contact; he "hacked to pieces" the land of Nubia, taking 7,000 captives and 200,000 cattle and sheep.

Merchants followed, moving deep into the country for donkey loads of ivory and leopard skins, ebony and incense. Ramesses the Great stocked his tomb with tons of gold from Egypt's backyard. And Egyptians set up forts, towns, temples, and boundary markers along the Nile almost as far south as the Fifth Cataract. In the cities of Kush, between Meroë and the Third Cataract, men built, worshiped, and governed in imitation of their northern neighbors.

Yet they were not always weaker. Eight hundred years before Christ, Kush was a powerful, independent kingdom. And Egypt, ruled for nearly two centuries by fair-skinned invaders from Libya, was falling to pieces. For the first time—and the last—the tide of human power turned down the Nile, against Egypt.

Kashta, King of Kush, marched north. Under his armies, the squabbling forces of

Out of desert sands rises the Archangel Michael near the banks of the Nile. The saint shields Shadrach, Meshach, and Abednego in the fiery furnace. This 1,000-year-old Coptic fresco adorned a cathedral in Faras, once the center of Christianity in Sudanese Nubia. Since its discovery in 1961, archeologists have saved some 100 priceless Nubian paintings.

Stylized scorpions by girl's head ward off real scorpions, according to an old belief in Egyptian Nubia. Before the Nile flooded her land, she also painted hens and flowers on her home.

GEORG GERSTER

southern Egypt crumbled. Kashta became first Pharaoh of the XXVth Dynasty. Piankhy came next. "Yoke the warhorses!" he commanded, "Draw up the battle line!" And the rest of Egypt fell. The people of Kush, called Ethiopians—"burnt faces"—by the Greeks, held an empire from Meroë to the Mediterranean.

But their dynasty was short. Assyrians came thundering out of their homeland in what is now northern Iraq, terrorizing the Middle East. Eventually they swept up the Nile and looted the fabulous city of Thebes itself. The Kushites, after less than a century of glory, fell back to the Fourth Cataract and their Sudanese capital of Napata. Not even there were they safe. Assyrians and mercenaries stormed the city for plunder. The king of Kush moved his capital to Meroë. And here, in the deep south of Nile civilization, the declining kingdom survived for the next thousand years.

In the Sudan, the city's ancient name now seems forgotten, confused with the present town of Merowe to the north. When we asked villagers along the road, they had never heard of the ruins. But mention Meroë to an archeologist and he thinks at once of pyramids.

Far better preserved than the ruined temples nearby, dozens of stone peaks poke up as though the desert were growing teeth. They are not so large as the massive pyramids near Cairo, which were more ancient to the Kushites than the Kushites are to us. Instead, they follow the shape of later pyramids at Thebes.

I climbed the steep, stepped walls of one of the largest—about 65 feet square, 60 feet high. Small stone chapels still stand in front of some, their walls alive with ancient citizens in tight, calf-length gowns.

Neither chapels nor pyramids held the royal remains. Dead kings, queens, and nobles of Kush went deep below the buildings, lowered into vertical shafts or carried down staircases cut into solid rock. In burial chambers at the bottom, they were sealed for eternity under rubble, plaster lime, and heavy slabs of sandstone and ironstone.

But their eternity lasted no longer than their kingdom. After the dynasty declined, robbers hacked into the underground passages. Wherever modern archeologists have probed among hundreds of pyramids along the Nile's great curve, they have found only remnants—jars, figurines, and gold that the plunderers missed. Of Kushite art, only fine reliefs remain, carved over outside walls, with crude camels of modern

NATIONAL GEOGRAPHIC PHOTOGRAPHER WINFIELD PARKS

Swinging sword and shield, a Nubian from the now flooded town of El Umbarakâb dances to honor an anniversary of a Moslem saint (left). After festivities, villagers take a sacred green cloth from the saint's tomb, board a brightly decorated boat, and cleanse the garment in the Nile (above). Woman (below) with tattooed lips wears a sparkling costume for the ceremony.

NATIONAL GEOGRAPHIC PHOTOGRAPHER WINFIELD PARKS

Anguish of farewell lines the faces of Nubians forced to evacuate Wadi Halfa. At the railway station, a woman balances a handwoven basket filled with household possessions. The town in the Sudan now lies beneath Lake Nasser.

origin that shepherds have scratched among the ancient sculptures.

Bumping away from Meroë in the morning, a truck can reach Atbara by lunchtime. At this tidy town of gardens and tree-shaded streets, the Nile gets its final transfusion before washing into one of the world's hottest deserts. But only in due season.

The Atbara River does not flow in midwinter. The sun tortures the earth at 110° F.; the stream becomes a chain of stagnant pools. By June, these are rarely a mile long, shallow communes for fish and turtles, crocodiles and hippopotamuses.

Then, in August, rainwater roars out of Ethiopia. Overnight, the Atbara swells a thousand feet wide, swirling with smashed bamboo, logs, whole trees still green. With this final contribution, rivers from the Ethiopian highlands give the Nile 86 percent of the water that reaches Egypt during the year. And without their gift, Nubia and Egypt would die.

Just north of Atbara, the river, road, and rail tracks move into land where years can pass without rain. Here true desert begins. Only at the Mediterranean shore does it end—except where the river brings life. The Nile itself flows on without a single significant tributary for 1,700 miles.

In the rock-strewn wilderness beyond Abu Hamed, the river veers west and south before curving toward Egypt again. Trucks and trains leave it and make a dash directly for the Egyptian frontier. I took an ivory-colored train. My coach had a double roof and shutters at the blue glass windows for protection against the sun, yet I recorded afternoon temperatures between 107° and 113° F. A clean shirt hung up for a few minutes felt as hot as one newly ironed when I put it on.

Dust devils frisk across the deathly land. Nothing of human significance lies along the way except the train stations, numbered from one to ten rather than named. At each stop, women and children sold sticks of sugar cane or tumblers of *lemoon*—lemonade. Near Station Six, a halting place for water, nomads had pitched tents of green canvas, camel hide, or yellow reed mats. As the train lurched, then rocked onward, black goats sprinted away from it and children in bright clothing ran along beside looking wistful, as if pursuing a dream.

The river, meanwhile, swings through a region that reminded Goddard of the Colorado River country of Utah. His party paddled through miles of hazard.

"We were never sure what danger lurked around the next bend," he said. "Once committed to a rapid, there was no turning back. Our open cockpits were so low that water nearly swamped us in every turbulent stretch, such as the steep Fourth Cataract."

Along this portion of the Nile, Nubian instead of Arabic is the daily language. Life is hard for these people. The river drowns their date gardens, the desert parches their wheat fields, and both combined produce

Mirrored by Lake Nasser, the mosque of Sayed El Hussein in Wadi Halfa slowly sinks below rising waters. Soon the lake will completely engulf the mosque and its towering minaret.

Caught in a flood path, Nubians leave their beloved homeland. Waiting forlornly for river transportation to a new village in the Kôm Ombo district, a Nubian (left) says goodbye to his dog. The ferry had room only for people, household goods, and farm animals.

Resembling the aftermath of a tidal wave, possessions clutter a sandstone bank (right) where a homeowner and his family await evacuation. The lake creeps higher; eventually it inundated the whitewashed mud houses.

Last residents of Dâbûd in the Sudan carry livestock as they leave the home of their ancestors. They load sheep aboard a felucca; cows stand benignly on deck. That part of Nubia from Aswân south into the Sudan's northern frontier vanished below Lake Nasser.

NATIONAL GEOGRAPHIC PHOTOGRAPHER WINFIELD PARKS

barely enough fruit and *kisra* cakes to keep them alive. Yet Nubians cling adamantly to their little domed villages.

Not only in modern times has this country been an island of tenacious tradition. Two centuries after the kingdom of Kush dwindled away, Nubians accepted Christianity from Byzantine rulers of Egypt. Only a century later, in 640, warriors from Arabia poured into North Africa, spreading the faith of Islam. Nubians were among the few peoples to resist. Despite Arab raids, kingdoms along the Nile's loop remained Christian for the next 800 years.

"I am not poor, O Cross that gives light," one of their songs began. A tenth-century manuscript, recently found in monastery ruins, preserves this as a hymn sung by Christ himself. Its translator, Dr. George R. Hughes of the University of Chicago's Oriental Institute, told me later: "We do not take that literally. But this prayer book shows how the Nubians worshiped before the Arabs made their country a land of Islam. Documents like this are treasures of history."

Nubia is a bonanza for scholars with shovels, and the recent spate of spadework there, an international effort, raced the waters that began to rise behind Aswân High Dam in 1964. Already the Nile spreads visibly. Much of Nubia in Egypt and the Sudan lies under a lake that will stretch 310 miles long and 14 miles wide after 1975.

Wadi Halfa, where the road and the rails meet the Nile again, held many thousands of Nubians a few years ago. For centuries, the Sudanese city had thrived as the traditional gateway for trade and travel between the Sudan and Egypt. I found the old town abandoned, drowned.

Gilbert M. Grosvenor, a NATIONAL GEOGRAPHIC editor, and his wife Donna caught one of the last glimpses of Nubian life here in 1964. Aboard Captain Irving Johnson's ketch *Yankee,* they sailed through the ancient land just before rising waters engulfed it completely.

They found women washing clothes in the river, boys driving donkeys through the powdered-rouge dust of the streets, and a man who talked jovially until someone mentioned the new lake and his eyes looked suddenly old.

Only weeks later the exodus began. Halfans had a lot to go to, a fine new life at

Doomed and deserted village in Egyptian Nubia soon will be lost forever under the sweeping expanse of Lake Nasser. The community with

NATIONAL GEOGRAPHIC PHOTOGRAPHER WINFIELD PARKS (ABOVE) AND R. G. RUSSELL

its white domed tomb of a local saint overlooked the Nile for centuries. Its residents packed their belongings and moved downriver to towns like new Dâbûd (below). The author views the resettlement village with Abdel Al Shahin, a government official of the Kôm Ombo area.

Khashm el Girba far to the southeast up the Atbara River. The Atbara, with a new dam and canals, would irrigate wheatfields, gardens, and orchards. The people themselves would have clean drinking water for the first time in their lives. New homes waited, with neighborhoods intact on streets named after the lanes of Wadi Halfa.

But what would become of 100,000 Nubians, uprooted by the creeping tide of progress? Those in the Sudan would go south; displaced Egyptian Nubians were evacuating 40 villages along 200 miles of the Nile and moving north to the Kôm Ombo region.

As *Yankee* sailed north, the Grosvenors saw them at the river's edge, waiting for steamers. "For the children this was an exciting adventure; for the aged it marked the end of a way of life," they noted in their journal. "But, dutifully, these people accept what comes as Allah's will.

"Steamers passed us with doors and windowframes stacked on deck—wood is a precious commodity. Family pets had to remain. Half-starved dogs and cats roamed frantically among deserted houses.

"We landed at a small village near sunset. Black doorways of empty houses stared out at us. Rounded roofs arched beside flat ones, each artistically decorated and terraced into the landscape overlooking the river. In one house, remnants of a child's shell collection lay tumbled from its box, forgotten in the bustle of the move.

"We stood on the hilltop as the full moon drenched the land in silver, and we knew what the Nubians would miss most: their glorious river.

"At Kôm Ombo the land is flat and monotonous, broken only by rows of identical houses. Here the Nubians no longer live beside the Nile. So far away is the river that even an evening's walk leaves them in the desert."

As steamers waited, the people of Nubia parted from relatives—parents, brothers, sisters, cousins—who lived across the border, then left a homeland behind. Water spilled into their villages in 1965, reaching Wadi Halfa by April.

A year later, I visited their new settlements in Egypt with Abdel Al Shahin, President of the Kôm Ombo Town Council. "The Nubians here are getting food from our government and the United States until new irrigation work is finished," he remarked as we drove north.

At the new village of Dâbûd I met Masloob Ali, an elderly man who spoke to me in fragmentary English. "When the dam is finished," I asked, "would you like to go back to old Nubia?"

"Oh, no," he laughed, "it's better here." He showed us a courtyard where girls were making clothing and bead necklaces for sale in Aswân. Then he took us to see his room—cool and clean, with a polished brass bed in one corner and pictures of his family and Egyptian movie stars hung and glued on the white walls.

Some people I met missed their old homes, and, as the Grosvenors predicted, the river most of all. Yet, however painful their memories, they seemed quite happy in the new villages of Kôm Ombo. And, here and there, I saw a house painted with traditional Nubian designs, or decorated with china dinner plates—gay symbols of acceptance that increase as an uprooted people make this area their home.

While much of Nubia was lost, many relics were saved. A National Geographic Society research grant helped archeologists uncover citadel walls, graveyards, and early Christian churches at Gebel Adda, a city occupied since the second century A.D. A 3,500-year-old temple that Queen Hatshepsut built at Buhen rumbled away on a train to Khartoum.

Temples at Kumna and Semna West went inland, stone by stone, to stand beyond reach of Lake Nasser. Five others were given to countries that helped finance salvage work. One, from Dandûr, will come to the United States. The Roman temple at Kalâbsha—13,000 stones averaging a ton apiece—sailed down the Nile on barges to a site near Aswân.

The masterpiece of all Nubian temples went up—straight up, to a cliff-ledge above the lake. In the salvation of Abu Simbel, men from many nations have woven a tale of ingenuity that would amaze the ancient pyramid builders.

Captains of toy tin boats, young Nubians sail the shallows of the Nile south of Aswân. Today these children can look to a future of improved educational facilities and higher living standards in their resettlement area of new Nubia.

8

MIGHTY WORKS OF MEN AND MONARCHS

CHUGGING NORTH THROUGH NUBIA, I saw a waterside ghost town 200 miles long. At the new Wadi Halfa, a cluster of plank huts where the railroad ends, I had booked passage on the little motor launch *Assouan.* As it eased away from the bank, it passed the old, submerged Wadi Halfa—the spire of a mosque and drowning palm trees still green.

Beyond, not even palms remained alive; nothing green met my eyes but the water of Lake Nasser. Sometimes we passed sandflats—more often, reddish bluffs or cliffs. On ledges still above water, mud houses stood in desolate silence.

At sunset I climbed to the roof of *Assouan*'s cabin to spend the night. Arab music wailed from radios below as I gazed into a moonless sky. Hot winds alternated with a cool breeze. About ten o'clock, a dome of light flared on the horizon—Abu Simbel, the only preserve of life along the way.

Scattered spotlights washed the scene with frosty brilliance and revealed enormous gray alcoves where gigantic temples once had stood—monuments to Ramesses II and his favorite consort Nefertari.

"This beautiful face," exclaimed a novelist in 1874 when she saw the sandstone portrait of Ramesses II, carved into the cliff at Abu Simbel in Egypt. Massive and majestic, the façade dwarfs a visitor to the Great Temple before its removal beyond the reach of rising Lake Nasser.

When *Yankee* passed here two years before, the temples still formed part of the cliff. "Nothing . . . could have prepared us for the thrill of that first sight of the towering stone colossi," the Johnsons said.

In 1874 an English novelist named Amelia Edwards gazed at the same overwhelming façade and noticed, as ladies will, dust on the mantel—in this case, lumps of white plaster pimpling the face of the colossus at the far right. An earlier visitor, making a cast of the statue, had left the residue. Amelia was disgusted by these "ghastly splotches" on "the most perfect face handed down to us by Egyptian art . . . one of the handsomest men . . . of all history."

She sent the crew of her houseboat scrambling aloft on an improvised scaffold to clean up the mess. The plaster left white stains in the porous brown stone, but Amelia took care of that with kitchen practicality and boudoir artifice. She ordered the men to brew buckets of strong coffee and give the Pharaoh a facial.

The United Arab Republic could have used some of Amelia's homely inventiveness about 85 years later. Water impounded by the Aswân High Dam would submerge Abu Simbel, and the government looked for ways to save the two temples here. Suggestions came cheap; price tags came as high as $90,000,000.

The engineers would have to move two temples literally carved out of the living

NATIONAL GEOGRAPHIC PHOTOGRAPHER WINFIELD PARKS

Inside the Great Hall, the sun spotlights one of eight pillarlike statues of Ramesses II. Here he proclaimed himself a god among gods. After reconstruction by highly skilled workmen, the temple will again appear as it has for centuries.

rock of a mountainside. The façade with its four colossal figures stood 110 feet high and 125 feet wide. The Great Hall, wide rooms, and inner sanctuary burrowed [illegible]00 feet into the mountain. The other temple, a shrine to Nefertari, was small only by comparison: 40 by 90 feet on the outside, 70 feet from entrance to back wall.

Early proposals called for cutting each temple out in one gigantic piece and raising it to the top of the cliff above, about the height of a 19-story building. The U.A.R. considered this and wisely tossed the problem to the world, through UNESCO, the United Nations Educational, Scientific and Cultural Organization. An intensive fund-raising campaign began, and more ideas to save the temples were solicited.

By 1963 the first phase of the dam was nearing completion, the water already rising. Forced to a decision, U.A.R. and UNESCO officials accepted a Swedish plan: Carve the monuments into manageable blocks, haul them away a block at a time, and reassemble them on the cliff top, at a cost of only $36,000,000.

Ramesses, were he alive today, would probably have taken the money and built another temple to himself somewhere else. Ruler of Egypt for 67 years after ascending the throne in 1304 B.C. (or, by another reckoning, 1290 B.C.), he achieved less in the way of conquest than he hoped

posterity would believe. But he won himself an enduring fame through architecture.

From the Delta to Nubia, a garland of temples, statues, and monuments proclaimed his renown. Of them all, Abu Simbel best captures the imperious spirit of the god-king. Here an inscription reads: "His Majesty commanded the making of a mansion in Nubia by cutting in the mountain. Never was the like done before except by the son of Amun."

As the *Assouan* plodded along through the dark, I could imagine his army of workmen, naked torsos glistening bronze and black under the blistering Nubian sun. They cling to the face of the rock on spidery scaffolds; they cut into it to remove ton after ton of stone. Draftsmen lay down the lines and squares just as the Pharaoh's architects have prescribed.

At the façade, stonecutters rough out four enormous figures of Ramesses II, his family at his feet. They carve the god Re-Harakhti over the entrance, a cornice of sacred baboons squatting above it to greet the rising sun.

Sculptors chip at the harsh outlines, smoothing them into dimpled lips three feet wide, legs and arms like tree trunks. Painters ply their fiber brushes dipped in vivid colors—the standard scheme of red, blue, yellow, white, and black.

Inside the Great Hall other sculptors

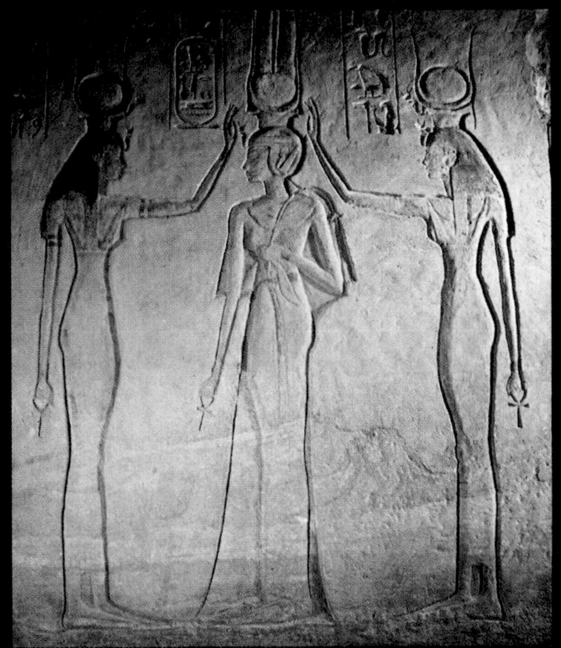

ROGER WOOD STUDIOS (ABOVE) AND GEORG GERSTER

Small Temple at Abu Simbel honors Ramesses' queen, "the great royal wife Nefertari." The Transverse Chamber wall preserves this graceful scene of goddesses Hathor and Isis placing an elaborate crown on Nefertari's head.

For 3,200 years the temples of Ramesses II (below, left) and his queen Nefertari (right) endured before craftsmen carved the shrines into sections, carefully moving each piece to safety. Raised 210 feet above this site and reassembled, the temples still share the Nile's west bank.

transform massive pillars into 30-foot statues of Ramesses as Osiris, king of the dead. They carve every inch of the walls into bas-reliefs which the painters finish, to show Ramesses in heroic victory against the Hittites, Ramesses talking with the gods, Ramesses a god among gods.

Deep in the sanctuary, architects and surveyors pay special attention to four gods seated on a common throne at the rear wall—Amun of Thebes, Re-Harakhti of Heliopolis, Ptah of Memphis, and Ramesses. With marvelous skill they orient the shrine so that twice a year, in October and February, rays of the rising sun will pierce the inner gloom to bathe in pure gold three of the throned figures. The fourth, Ptah, will live in eternal darkness.

EVEN IN THE TEMPLE dedicated to Nefertari and Hathor, goddess of love, figures of Ramesses dominate most of the walls. And according to the Greek historian Diodorus, the Pharaoh's colossal statue at Thebes bore the haughty inscription: "I am Osimanduas [Ramesses] King of Kings; if any would know how great I am . . . let him excel me in any of my Works."

Yet Abu Simbel, his proudest work, was completely forgotten. The attendant priests abandoned it. By 1000 B.C. the Egyptian empire had begun to decline. The Great Temple slumbered through succeeding centuries as the sands of the Western Desert billowed over it.

Nefertari's temple, facing a different direction and more protected from the prevailing winds, remained uncovered, and descriptions of it drifted down the Nile. In 1813 a wandering Swiss scholar named John Lewis Burckhardt came to see for himself and found the Small Temple "in complete preservation." He stood admiring the six statues on its façade—four of Ramesses bracketing two of his queen, with their children at their feet.

Then, quite by accident, he made his great discovery. In the distance, over a mountain of sand, he caught sight of "what is yet visible of four immense colossal statues"—the double crown, head, and part of the torso of one, the crowns of two others. The head of the fourth had fallen and lay buried in the sand.

From hasty calculations he guessed that the statues measured between 65 and 70

An army of artisans, following a standardized color scheme, completes details of the Great Temple's façade. A solar disk crowns the falcon-headed deity Re-Harakhti, who seems to stride out of the wall above the entrance. Beneath his right hand, sculptors carved User, the jackal-headed staff; and, beneath his left (obscured by

PAINTING BY ROBERT W. NICHOLSON, NATIONAL GEOGRAPHIC ARTIST

overseers), the figure of Maat, goddess of truth. The triumvirate represents User-maat-re, Rammesses' coronation name. The Pharaoh in bas-relief on either side thus presents offerings not only to the god, but to himself. Wind-blown sand weathered and scoured the temple face of its vivid colors. When waters of Lake Nasser threatened the temples of Abu Simbel, salvagers dismantled them into 1,060 keyed and numbered blocks. In repositioning the temples on the heights above, workmen put the colossal blocks back into place as precisely as parts in a fine watch. Craftsmen cut seams less than a quarter of an inch wide, leaving only thin scars visible.

feet high. "... I suspect," he wrote, "could the sand be cleared away, a vast temple would be discovered. . . ."

Burckhardt guessed correctly. But he never saw the temple excavated; he died of dysentery in Egypt in 1817. In that same year an Italian engineer-adventurer named Giovanni Battista Belzoni began digging out Abu Simbel, hoping to find valuable antiquities.

Shoveling the sand was like "making a hole in the water," Belzoni reported. Only after much backbreaking work could he and his helpers enter the temple. Inside, perspiration dripping off their fingers stained their sketchbooks. But by the flickering light of candles and torches they gazed on a sight that had been sealed from the eyes of men for almost 3,000 years—in Belzoni's words, "one of the most magnificent of temples, enriched with beautiful intaglios, painting, colossal figures. . . ."

Sand remained a problem, however. As fast as men shoveled it away, more blew over the entrance. Finally, diversion walls built in 1892 helped thwart it. Ironically, when salvage operations got under way in 1964, workmen began by piling a massive shield of sand—more than 5,000 truckloads of it—around the statues to protect them from falling stone.

By this time the river was already licking up the narrow bank in front of the temples. Engineers put up a cofferdam 80 feet high, borrowing time—the river would not spill over its top until mid-August, 1966.

An international group of contractors formed Joint Venture Abu Simbel: French, Italian, Egyptian, and Swedish firms led by Hochtief of West Germany. Supervising the work were the Egyptian government and the Swedish firm that had drawn up the plan, Vattenbyggnadsbyrån, or VBB. And now the sightless eyes of Abu Simbel's statuary looked out on a burst of activity rivaling the days of their creation.

A babel of tongues cursed the Egyptian heat as hundreds of men from many nations got to work. They probed the sandstone to test its inner tensions and shored up the interiors with steel scaffolding. They gouged out the mountain behind the temples to the sound of whining winches and clanking cranes, to the hoarse rumble of bulldozers, to the stutter of pneumatic hammers and drills.

Marmisti—skilled stonecutters from Italy's marble quarries—took up the task when the mountain had been stripped away to within 31 inches of the temple walls and ceilings. They sawed the shrines into manageable chunks of 20 and 30 tons. Engineers prescribed injections and sprays of plastic resin to strengthen the friable sandstone. But the marmisti were confident. "We know rocks like hearts," one said. "We know when they break."

Of eight miles of roads in the area, only one stretch was paved—between the old temple site and the cliff-top storage yard. Abu Simbel's dismembered pieces were hauled gently up the hill in trucks with sand-cushioned beds. The fragile stone could not take jouncing; people could.

Albert Papenburg, a young German liaison officer for Joint Venture Abu Simbel, told me about the work's progress when I met him in Aswân.

"All in all," he said, "we lifted 1,060 blocks. We heaved up the last one in April, 1966, after working around the clock for a

Awed visitor, novelist Amelia Edwards studies the throne wall of Ramesses' temple in February, 1874. She found a beam of sunlight reaching 200 feet into the sanctuary, shining on Ramesses and his fellow gods. Sunlight will still fall on them each February and October even though the temple stands on higher ground.

PAINTINGS BY ROBERT W. NICHOLSON, NATIONAL GEOGRAPHIC ARTIST

Covered by a sea of sand, the Great Temple lay concealed for almost 3,000 years. In 1817 Giovanni Battista Belzoni (above) dug away 31 feet of sand to reach the door. He found "one of the most magnificent of temples, enriched with . . . intaglios, painting, colossal figures. . . ."

year. We've laid concrete foundations for the temples, and most of the rooms are finished already. By the end of 1966 the temples will be completely rebuilt."

"Then you'll go home?" I wondered.

"Oh, no. In 1967 we're going to build concrete domes over the temples. That's to hold the weight of the cliff we're going to erect above the temples, to keep the setting as it was. It's the original cliff, you know. We took that too."

Exact orientation of the Great Temple will still allow the sun to aim its golden floodlight on Ramesses in his hidden sanctuary twice a year. Even the tumbled head of the broken statue outside will once more bury its face in the sand at its own feet.

Before the cliff is finished, a hotel will open west of the new temple site. Discovery of Abu Simbel had brought a dribble of tourists up the Nile. Interest in the salvage brought a wave. Now Egyptian officials hope for a flood.

Today you can fly from Cairo to Aswân, hop on a hydrofoil, and be within camera range of the temples in five hours. These waterbugs skim up and back the same day, with a stopover an hour and a half long. Other vessels make more leisurely trips.

My little *Assouan*, moving north toward

Aswân, made about six knots. Each morning her canteen served soy beans, very black Turkish coffee, and very sweet tea for breakfast. All afternoon I perched comfortably on the gunwale, dipping my shirt every so often to put it on wet and cool.

Goddard and his friends spent two months paddling from Khartoum to Aswân. "From dawn to dusk," he wrote, "stroking down the pale-green Nile, we sweltered under the savage African sun. . . . At times the heat seemed to have physical consistency, like a fiery fog. Around midday, with the temperature at 125° or higher in the shade, it was painful even to breathe." They drank an average 12 quarts of Nile water per man per day, he reported, and "no beverage ever tasted so delicious."

The *Assouan* served Nile water too, filtered through cheesecloth. It tasted fresh, but only desert thirst and powerful imagination could make it seem fit to drink.

In the wider reaches of Lake Nasser, I noticed an extreme humidity that disappeared whenever we came near the shore—uncomfortable proof of evaporation from the new desert lake. But despite this loss to the sun, the water brims up to make the High Dam a "wall against hunger," as one expert has called it.

Ninety-nine percent of Egypt's 29 million people live on just four percent of the country's 386,000 square miles—on a shoestring of cultivation along the Nile. The dam will provide a wash of green for an additional million acres of barren yellow, increasing the nation's crop-producing land by nearly one-third.

In Aswân I met Abdel Aziz Eid, Acting Deputy Director of Public Relations for the High Dam, who told me that the body of the dam will be finished by 1968. "In the power station," he said, "three turbines will be working by 1967; all 12 will be in operation by early 1970." The generators will spin out ten billion kilowatt hours of electricity annually to power a new surge of industry for Egypt. Above all, the dam will parcel out water saved from fat years to nourish the lean.

Lake Nasser drowns Nubia but promises a bounty. Precious storage water will reclaim a million acres from Egypt's deserts, and increase the crops produced on an additional 700,000 acres from one to three each year.

GEORG GERSTER

Another High Dam official, Fathi Allam, took me to visit the site. From a lookout point above the unfinished power station, I saw men scrambling over immense shapes of concrete and steel. The Nile ran under them, unseen, through a single sluice gate, and emerged in green whirlpools.

We crossed the body of the dam. More than two miles long and almost a mile thick at its base, it will have room for a highway 131 feet wide along the crest. Below us, groaning trucks dumped loads of rocks that looked like teaspoonfuls as they tumbled down the gargantuan man-made slopes.

Ramesses would have approved of *Sadd el Aali*, the High Dam: It is being built to his scale. When completed, it will contain almost 55 million cubic yards of material—enough for 17 Great Pyramids.

Moving a mountain to move a giant, engineers cut away rock around the temples, leaving only a shell (left). Stonecutters sawed the rock into 20- and 30-ton slabs. Cranes lifted pieces (right) into cushioned trailers bound for storage. Painting (below) shows the old location of temples under Lake Nasser and their new cliff-top site.

PAINTING BY ROBERT W. NICHOLSON, NATIONAL GEOGRAPHIC ARTIST (BELOW) AND GEORG GERSTER

Hydroelectric power station at the Sadd el Aali—*the Aswân High Dam—nears completion. The dam will fulfill Egypt's dream of saving water from the fat years to provide for the lean.*

NATIONAL GEOGRAPHIC PHOTOGRAPHER JOSEPH J. SCHERSCHEL

Just as Ramesses' servants did, some workmen here carry earth and stone in baskets. But they have help from Swedish rock drills, American bulldozers, huge British excavators, and Russian trucks so monstrous a driver must climb a ladder to reach the cab. The U.S.S.R. is financing the project and providing more than 800 engineers and technicians to guide the work. But Sadd el Aali will not be a "Russian" dam: The work force of 30,000 includes men from many nations, among them Finland, Switzerland, India, Ghana, Canada, Argentina, and the United States.

RETURNING TO ASWÂN by way of the west bank, we drove about five miles downstream to cross the Nile again on the old dam, "el Khazzan," built by British engineers and Egyptian workmen in 1902, later improved twice to increase its height.

There I could see Philae Island, with orange machinery on barges floating above its half-drowned shrines. Since 1902, few travelers have seen these splendid Ptolemaic and Roman temples, for they lay like sunken ships on the floor of the reservoir. Only in summer did they emerge into sunlight, when the sluice gates of the old dam opened to release the silt-laden waters of the flood.

Now three dikes, designed by the Dutch and financed by the United States, will keep the island dry all year round. Soon visitors may stroll there once more, as perhaps Cleopatra did. When its palms and acacias grow again, they can see why Philae acquired the name "Pearl of Egypt."

Downstream from Philae and the dam, the Nile swirls around the glistening granite boulders of the First Cataract, where Egyptian engineers had cleared a channel by 2330 B.C. They cut around the biggest mound of rock, Elephantine Island.

In Old Kingdom days the island's strategic position gave it a role and a name: "Door to the South." The conquerors who have passed here since have left their mark on Elephantine, although many of their monuments are nothing but rubble now: the temple to Khnum, ram-headed god of the cataract, and the temple built by the Roman Emperor Trajan.

But the most important relic is a stairway of hewn stones leading down into the river—Elephantine's Nilometer, used in pharaonic times to record the height of the flood. From this device and others like it, officials calculated taxes for the year.

On the eastern shore opposite Elephantine, Aswân spreads back from the river. Since Edwardian days, wealthy and thin-blooded refugees from Europe's harsh winters have known Aswân as a quiet resort. But now, I think, the town must be the most dynamic in Egypt. A new boulevard curves along the river, with silvery streetlights and pink granite curbstones. Everywhere the scent of fresh concrete and plaster wafts along on hot Nile gusts from the north. Laborers positively run with sacks of cement on their backs and baskets of sand on their heads. Steel mills and chemical plants are going up, and the press calls the city the "Pittsburgh of Egypt."

But strolling inland, past the new air-conditioned buildings, I entered the Arabian Nights: crowded, dusty bazaars, crumbling houses of mud brick. Along one quiet old street, a passer-by stopped to greet me. He kissed my hand and called me pasha. He remembered the manners of another age better than those of the present.

When ancient Egypt declined, Aswân still lived, converted into a military camp by the Romans. Greeks, Turks, Frenchmen, and Englishmen all had their turns, and ruined stones still bear carved names—Marcus, Mahmud, Michel, and Mac.

Through it all, Aswân retained a link with her ancient masters and their gods. She holds it still, wherever Egypt's time-worn relics stand—by the Nile, or in a museum half a world away. From her quarries came enduring granite. In a country of sand and mud it symbolized eternity.

Late one afternoon, I walked a mile or so out to the dusty tan valley of the quarry. Hot winds hummed through the silence. All around I found deep notches on great rock walls. Egyptian quarrymen had cut them, placing wedges of wood in the depressions and wetting the wood to make it swell and split the rock. Obelisks, statues, and building stones came from this quarry. The Nile carried them downriver, to the Pharaohs' grandest cities.

Streaked with a scarring flaw and abandoned by the ancients, this granite obelisk measures 137 feet in length and about 14 feet thick at its base. Author visits the quarry near Aswân, source of granite for many temples and tombs.

9

TEMPLES AND GODS

ABOUT 450 YEARS before Christ, a restless Greek scholar sailed from his home at Halicarnassus, on the Turkish coast, and toured the civilized lands around the Mediterranean. An inquisitive man, Herodotus roamed up the Nile all the way to the First Cataract to see what he could "with my own eyes."

Many of the things he saw and recorded in his books I found too. Egyptian temples and tombs have suffered far less from time than other remains of the ancient world. And the valley of the Nile looks much as it did when huge barges were casting off from Aswân with 300-ton granite obelisks bound for the city of Thebes.

Casting off more modestly in a small rented felucca named *Mary*, I drifted into the deep serenity that wanderers have always found here. Morning sun sizzles over the water as the sail snaps and bulges taut. The river sweeps along with a sumptuous sliding motion, snatching the boat the moment the stern line splashes free. The boatman steers almost to midstream, then bears right to follow other triangles of patched canvas, vague shapes in a light like mist squeezed from lemons.

Monumental majesty of Luxor recalls the golden age of Egypt's power under Amenophis III in the 14th century B.C. Here dwelt Amun, mightiest of gods. Hundreds of slaves served him within the 853-foot-long temple.

Whenever the boat skims toward the bank, women crouching on beaches of yellow sand look up, then avert their eyes as they plunge clay pots to gulp the Nile. They adjust little cotton doughnuts on their heads, balance the jars on them, and trudge to mud-walled homes.

Farm animals shuffle along the bank, nearly buried under loads of cane for thatch or dates bundled in nets. Donkeys probably ambled here when history began; many authorities believe they originally came from Egypt. Oxen turned waterwheels for the Pharaohs. Only the camel is new, as Egypt knows newness; it appeared as a beast of burden only when Persians conquered the land in 525 B.C.

The land beyond the bank holds many shades of green, a patchwork of sugarcane, vegetables, and grains. Squares of black wait for planting. Nearly always the desert is in sight—a shriek of brilliance between palms and tamarisks.

Every few miles, the boatman points to the bank and grates out an Arabic village name: "El Khaṭṭâra," with the first two letters scraped over the back of his palate . . . "El ʿAqaba el Saghîra . . . El ʿAqaba el Kebîra." Between here and Cairo, thousands of mud cubes with teacup domes cluster on the edge of dazzling desert like ceramics baking in a kiln.

Beyond the villages, wasteland almost empty covers 96 percent of the country.

River people ignore it; for them, most of Egypt is a nation they can walk across in part of a leisurely morning.

The next cloudy day can be three years away in parts of Egypt, and sunset burns over the desert nearly every evening. In the last reddish light on the Nile, huge sails look like pink orchid petals. Then, suddenly, they wither. Boatmen aboard the big cargo *naggars* cling to yards that rise 130 feet above the water. Clenching their robes between their teeth, they gather canvas hand over hand. With sails furled tight, they will pray and rest and talk quietly before their evening meal.

A small felucca like mine, easier to handle, merely brushed the bank. Secured under full sail to a water-worn root, it fluttered like a moth as we wandered inland to bargain for food. The boatman led the way, hopping little irrigation canals. We followed a path along dikes that held Nile water in big square basins where maize, clover, and sorghum soon would grow.

When the boatman sighted the two-room hut of a *fellah,* or farmer, he asked me to wait outside; foreigners have a reputation for paying what is asked and spoiling the sport of a good bargain. Looking victorious, he emerged with a victorious-

NATIONAL GEOGRAPHIC PHOTOGRAPHER WINFIELD PARKS

Temple to honor Horus, hawk-headed god and special patron of the Pharaohs, soars above a playing field at Idfu, on the west bank of the Nile half way between Aswân and Luxor. Huge pylon marks the entrance to the shrine, completed 2,000 years ago and most perfectly preserved of Egyptian ruins.

Dark blade skimming, a turbaned barber in the Idfu market attends a client. In the distance beyond him rises the great sandstone pylon.

Sacred falcon, one of a pair carved in granite, guards the entrance. In the relief on the wall appear a Pharaoh (left) and Horus.

looking farmer and they browsed around the hut with palm-frond baskets.

They put oranges in the bottom, grapes to one side; then they shuffled into a cave of leaves for bananas and mangoes. "*Mazbut? Ziyada?*" the farmer asked. He brought out jars of coffee either sweet or very sweet, depending on the answer. On top of the basket-load went a bunch of fresh red dates with meat as white and crispy as coconut.

After dinner, I went to work for my boatman. I curled up in the bow of the felucca, navigating by pale domes of village light that flared on the horizon ahead. Nile boats carry no lights as a rule, so I listened for the whisper of water off other prows and peered into the blackness for ghostly gliding shapes.

The moon over dry desertland rises as naked as a peeled apple, and the river suddenly becomes a glinting highway. When the stream narrows the boatman knows he has reached Idfu. Not far from the bank, an angular eruption of stone soars above the village, looking in the moonlight much as it did 2,000 years ago.

The temple of Horus has deteriorated only slightly since Pharaohs of the Ptolemy line built it between 237 and 57 B.C. The twin wedge-shaped towers of the entrance pylon rise 110 feet from the hard desert floor. Ptolemy Auletes and his hawk-headed god still stride in frozen motion over the outer walls—giants in incised relief. Beyond the pylon, however, in long columned halls, many carved figures have lost their faces. Early Christians, anxious to be rid of old ideas, hacked them away.

The next day is like every day on the Nile—tied to eternity. The river slides on like liquid sand. Mist dissolves and the sky turns to marble. It has always been like this. At every bend shadoofs measure out the hours like seesaw pendulums, and sakiehs turn as deliberately as clock gears.

From sunrise to dusk, a shadoof can water an eighth of an acre. It bobs up and down like a toy drinking bird—a long wooden boom with weights on one end, jars or buckets or cans on the other. For hours on end, a farmer seesaws the boom on its triangular fulcrum.

With a sakieh, a boy and a water buffalo can do the work of several shadoofs. The loinclothed lad prods his blindfolded animal round and round, turning a large cogged wheel. Geared to that, a vertical wheel dips pots into a ditch dug to river level. It dumps them into a higher ditch that runs inland.

Triple shadoof lifts life-giving Nile water to a field. A pole with a weight on one end and a pot or bucket dangling from the other, this irrigation device, familiar to the ancients, still creaks beside the river from the Sudan to the Delta.

EVEN INNOVATIONS have a measure of eternity about them. Egypt now has some 250,000 Archimedes screws—hand-cranked spirals, boxed in wood, that raise water as barbershop poles raise stripes. Ramesses would not recognize these, but Cleopatra would. The chronic cough of gasoline pumps should break the spell of endlessness, but the engines only maintain it in their own way, one coming into hearing as the one before it fades.

Imaginative writers have said the Nile maintained one of the world's longest continuous civilizations because there is little here to suggest change. And how long did that civilization endure? If classical Greece had lasted until the present day her culture would not yet be as old. Ancient Egypt remained fairly well intact throughout the 3,100 years before Christ was born.

King Menes, according to tradition, became the first monarch to rule all Egypt when he unified the "Two Lands"—the Valley and the Delta. He built a fortress called the "White Wall," and it grew into the capital city of Memphis. His successors built the pyramids nearby—palaces for their personal eternities. And for centuries it seemed as if their Egypt, which we call the Old Kingdom, was itself eternal.

Then it collapsed. The provinces rebelled in 2130 B.C. From a period of anarchy rose Egypt's most splendid city, called Weset by its own people, Thebes by the Greeks.

The kings from Thebes put Egypt together again, and kept it together through many of the next one thousand years. Today the ruins of their city make up the largest outdoor museum in the world.

On a present-day map, the main part of Thebes bears two names. The city faded along with ancient Egypt, but people remained here, building villages within the crumbling walls. They called their settlements *Al Uqşur* and *El Karnak*—"the Castles" and "the Fortress." At the first of these, a sizable town now known as Luxor, I left my felucca and climbed the bank to a delightful quayside boulevard.

Tidy trees rose along the road like big green mushrooms, each shading a sprinkle of winter flowers. Horse-drawn carriages clattered by, warning goats and cloaked pedestrians with chimes instead of horns. To end the day, Luxor's birds celebrated sunset with chimes almost as loud and a water truck honked by, spraying down the dust of a hot afternoon.

Within easy walking distance from the river, I found a charming antique hostelry with gardens, pillared ceilings, Oriental furniture, and grandfatherly brass beds well polished and canopied under mosquito netting. That evening, I dined on a terrace overlooking the ruins of a temple.

Beyond a spray of palm fronds, the columns, pylons, and walls looked like cast bronze as the sun poured its last light over them. The whole silent temple floated on a sunken lake of shadow. A muezzin's chant called the faithful to evening prayer, and the ruins faded—then reappeared under dim blue spotlights.

The Middle Kingdom monarchs who ruled Egypt from Thebes after 2040 B.C. would not recognize the buildings that we see here today. They had temples of their own, but those became stone quarries for other builders after a second period of weakness and civil strife gave birth to the New Kingdom about 1567 B.C.

This third great period lifted the nation to a pinnacle of civilization, to mastery of an empire reaching from Nubia in the south to Syria in the north. Coming to the throne in this triumphant time, Pharaohs of the XVIIIth and XIXth Dynasties wanted new temples—larger and grander ones to show the might and wealth that made their capital, as they said proudly, "Mistress of Every City."

Amenophis III commanded the present Luxor temple into existence about 1400

Twenty centuries of construction, another 20 of decay, form the history of the temple of Amun at Karnak. Many Pharaohs paid homage to their gods and themselves with monumental additions. Huge First Pylon (far right) leads to Hypostyle Hall of Ramesses II. Obelisk honors Hatshepsut, female Pharaoh.

ELIOT ELISOFON

B.C. to honor Amun, the god of Weset, his wife Mut, and their son Khonsu. But, like all of Thebes, this temple was under construction for a long time—most of the next millennium, in fact. The square courtyard Amenophis laid out within a forest of pillars is now only the center of the edifice.

Tutankhamun decorated a columned corridor some time during the next century. Ramesses II added a pylon after another century. Alexander the Great ordered a new sanctuary when the building was 1,100 years old. Today, Amun's partially restored temple is 853 feet long, considerably longer than St. Peter's Basilica.

But, through all the additions, it remained considerably smaller than Amun's mammoth monument at Karnak, a mile and a half to the northeast. In more leisurely days, wealthy Europeans wintering at Luxor would hail a carriage and clop off to Karnak by moonlight. I chose an evening luminous with haze and did the same.

The desert night often grows cool, and foreign women browsing waterfront shops wore fur stoles. Above them, on wooden latticed balconies, Egyptian women sat bundled from head to foot in black. The carriage chimed through a traffic of camels, cabs, and donkeys. A merchant trotted beside it for a moment, holding out a fine ivory figurine of Pharaoh Sethos I; that afternoon I had seen him carving it by hand, using a postcard picture as his pattern.

Down the block, I noticed boys perched along curbstones like birds on a telephone wire. I stopped the driver to investigate. With no electricity at home, they were studying their schoolbooks under the streetlights. Some of them asked me, as boys here have always asked tourists, for chocolate, or "cigarette for papa." But most of them wanted the ballpoint pens in my shirt pocket—"for school."

The town wraps itself around the riverbank ruins, and at a word the coachman snapped his whip and turned into an old

Excursion craft, patterned on boats shown in ancient tomb paintings, glides past Nilometer at Elephantine Island. Steps of hewn stone (behind wall) measured the river's annual rise. Nilometer readings governed pharaonic taxes: the higher the flood, the higher the levy.

NATIONAL GEOGRAPHIC PHOTOGRAPHER JOSEPH J. SCHERSCHEL

Feet held high, a bicyclist avoids a sprinkling from a water wagon laying the dust of Luxor. Known to Homer as Thebes, this city in its days of power styled itself Weset, "the pattern for every city." One inscription declares: "Both the flood and the earth were in her from the beginning of time . . . mankind came into being within her. . . ."

In Luxor's marketplace, a black-garbed vendor haggles over a white pigeon. Tomb paintings reveal the ancient Thebans as a pleasure-loving people, given to elaborate dinner parties enlivened by flutes, harps, and dancing girls. One song: "Come, songs and music are before thee; set behind thee all cares; think only upon gladness."

Animals of Egypt—sheep, donkeys, camels—come with their masters to modern Luxor on Tuesday, market day. Shepherds bring their thick-fleeced flocks, then squat patiently while awaiting buyers. Beast of burden in this region for thousands of years, a donkey plods along under a load of new earthenware pots; housewives will use them to carry water from the Nile to their mud-brick homes. Camels with their workaday loads shuffled onto the scene in comparatively recent centuries—after invaders from Persia conquered Egypt in 525 B.C.

NATIONAL GEOGRAPHIC PHOTOGRAPHER JOSEPH J. SCHERSCHEL

shopping center. A few robed men had brought stools to a streetlamp, and they chatted under a huge, very dry crocodile fastened over the door of an antiquities shop. A few yards farther, two youths were weaving cane armchairs in a blot of kerosene light. An icy stick of fluorescence clung to the ceiling of a barbershop, and turbans hung on a knobby Victorian hat rack. Eerie firelight flared from an open-front shop where boys scooped bread trays from an oven with thin wooden paddles.

The horse turned back toward the river at the far end of the Luxor ruins, where the minaret of Abu el Haggag Mosque jabs upward like a pointed pillar. The mosque rose within the walls of an early Christian church, which in turn rose within the temple courtyard of Ramesses II.

Tired old villas brood along the riverbank, all their peeling shutters closed. Pashas and beys once took tea in the gardens around them, now gone to weeds. Egypt has abolished both landlords and their titles. A man may own 104 acres, but no more. Well farmed, that yields the equivalent of $6,000 a year, not enough for luxurious winters in Luxor.

Near the ruins of Karnak, the center of ancient Thebes, mud huts cluster where those of commoners probably stood 3,500 years ago. No one really knows what their homes looked like. Along with the mud-brick palaces of the Pharaohs, the dwellings dissolved into the land. Nile fellahin still lay out gray bricks of mud and chopped straw to dry, just as ancient farmers did. And there is no reason to doubt that they stack the bricks the same way when they build their simple rectangular homes.

Temples, on the other hand, were built for eternity. For the monstrous palace of worship here, the architects used mostly sandstone, thousands of tons of it. Block by block, twin towers of a massive pylon rise overhead, each 142 feet tall. A gate between them leads into a maze of many courtyards and buildings. I wandered through this confusion of stone for days. Karnak sprawls over 60 acres. And it took more than 2,000 years to build.

It was never quite finished. Just inside the first pylon—the newest one, planned about 950 B.C. by the Libyan Pharaoh Sheshonk I—a construction ramp of crumbling mud bricks leans against the wall as it has for centuries. While this pylon grew, Egypt was dying.

But it was very much alive, and at the peak of its splendor, when the Hypostyle Hall went up about 1300 B.C. Moving across a vast open courtyard, I entered this dim stone forest. Hypostyle, a Greek term, means "resting on pillars." Here, stone roof slabs many tons in weight rest 79 feet off the ground on an array of 134 columns. Architects of Sethos I lighted the hall with small windows high above. Chambers beyond grew progressively darker, smaller, farther from the sun-flooded world of men. How better to capture the mystery of Amun, whose name means "Hidden"?

EGYPTIAN ARCHITECTS often built on a gargantuan scale: Karnak's Hypostyle Hall alone could hold the Cathedral of Notre Dame of Paris with room to spare. But they caught the essence of simplicity in form. Pylons stand like pairs of blunt wedges. Halls are plain rectangles. Columns imitate the simple forms of nature as Nile-dwellers knew it—sculpted papyrus sheaves and lotus stems holding up capitals of papyrus blossoms and lotus buds in stone.

The more I wandered in the ruins—climbing pylons, circling columns, hopping over scattered stones—the more I noticed color. Bits of brightness clung to walls and pillars. Recalling hues better preserved in ancient tombs, I could envision temple colors as well: blue and green, yellow and black, white and a rather unpleasant red, the shades of gumdrops.

When the colors were fresh, temples must have been as joyous, as summery, as a beach tent. And towering columns, gay with patterns, must have seemed to float, like long plastic balloons.

Sunrise at Thebes 3,000 years ago splashed over a dazzling city. Spangles of light shot from gold-capped square pillars that Greeks, in awed good humor, called obelisks—"little roasting spits." Stark white plaster covered temple walls where brilliantly painted reliefs did not, and huge ornamented doors glittered in the pylons. Gardens spread around the buildings. And inside, where only priests and divine Pharaohs could go, yellow stars shone in a heaven of blue ceilings. I could still see those, but gold and semiprecious stones that once embellished inner walls disappeared long ago. After the reign of Ramesses III, who died about 1167 B.C., the splendor of Thebes began to slip away, along with the might of all Egypt. But the city survived long after that, dwindling slowly into a provincial town. In the second century after Christ, sculptors were still carving decorations on the temples.

By A.D. 400, however, the great shrines of Amun sheltered churches and huts within their walls. And villagers were chipping away the strange pagan patterns they no longer understood.

Not quite everything was forgotten. To this day, and for as long as anyone in Luxor can remember, people of the town have celebrated a gay festival once every year. It begins when a boat, bright with paint and banners, rumbles on a wheeled cart to the head of a procession. More carts line up, each one full of streamers, flowers, and children. Someone starts a cheer and the parade slowly moves forward. The marchers sing hymns as they circle the walls of Luxor temple.

"What does the procession honor?" a visitor inquires.

This is the feast of Abu el Haggag, they say, a Moslem saint who came from Baghdād and converted Christian Luxor to Islam many centuries ago. The sacred boat is Abu el Haggag's.

After the procession, the stranger can stroll into the temple and see the festival all over again. In the colonnade decorated by Tutankhamun, ancient Thebans stand stiffly on the walls, cheering over the Nile. A sacred boat, carried on a barge, is making its yearly journey from the main temple at Karnak to the southern temple at Luxor. But this boat shrine belongs to the great god Amun.

A forest of pillars, Karnak's Hypostyle Hall towers 79 feet above the temple floor. Reliefs depicting kings and gods ring the columns, each 33 feet around. Obelisk erected by Queen Hatshepsut punctuates an adjoining part of the temple.

10

SECRET VALLEY OF THE KINGS

BY ROYAL COMMAND, the architect Ineni roamed into deathly desert hills west of Thebes. He was searching for a place where dead kings could lie forever among the golden treasures of their tombs.

Thutmosis I had sent him on this errand of eternity. By 1520 B.C., when this XVIIIth Dynasty monarch ruled the empire, everyone knew that the strongest pyramid could not protect a royal mummy and its rich provisions from the greed of thieves. And, like all Egyptian kings, Thutmosis wanted his body entombed securely so his *ka,* or spiritual twin, would find it, enter it, and restore him to joyous life in the afterworld. Only a secret crypt could defend him.

In the desolate hills Ineni found a perfect place, a valley about five miles west of the Nile. "I attended to the excavation of the cliff-tomb of His Majesty alone," the architect related on the walls of his own tomb, "no one seeing, no one hearing."

In centuries that followed, the lonely gorge became a honeycomb of man-made caves, a graveyard for monarchs until the end of the XXth Dynasty. Perhaps no spot on earth has held greater riches than the place we call Valley of the Kings.

Golden splendor gleams from the visage of King Tutankhamun on his third or innermost coffin. His funeral treasure, buried with him 1,340 years before Christ, came to light when an archeologist found the tomb in 1922.

Every morning, ferryboats from Luxor gurgle over the Nile. Astern, the wide, green Theban plain lies under a powder of mist. But the country ahead looks crisp and bright. Beyond a flat strip of shoreland only two and a half miles wide, the Western Desert leaps straight up in brilliant tan cliffs hundreds of feet high.

A narrow road runs between sunken basins of farmland. When canals bring water for planting season, white egrets come to rest in the shiny pools. Fellahin splash over the countryside. Here and there, trees shiver with every whisper of cool wind.

Life ends suddenly. Rich soil collides head-on with yellow desert, and not a single shrub crosses the border. But the road does. In glaring foothills, rocks, huts, and cliffs seem to vibrate in the heat. Here more than 3,000 years ago a splendid city arose.

The dead demanded much in ancient Egypt. Ornate tombs were only the beginning. Pharaohs set aside huge estates to endow temples where elaborate rituals would keep their memory alive. Early mortuary temples stood near the tombs they served. But if the Valley of the Kings was to remain secret, its tomb-temples, full of priests, scribes, guards, and custodians, could not stand too near. While kings went to rest in the desert, the city of temples spread out in full view of the Nile.

I turned aside into a short valley called Deir el Bahri, to see one of these shrines, the temple for a king who was a lady.

Hatshepsut, daughter of Thutmosis I, did not inherit his throne. Judging from hieroglyphs, she could not: The only word for "queen" means "king's great wife," implying that women did not rule countries. Instead, she married her half-brother, Thutmosis II, becoming his queen. Then he died. Hatshepsut had no son, so the child of her husband and a palace concubine was crowned Thutmosis III, Lord of the Two Lands. Hatshepsut became the power behind the throne as regent for the child Pharaoh.

But a few years later she defied custom and declared that the great god Amun had come forth from his temple and chosen her to be "king." The story hints of political fraud, but it won the throne for her. One of the first ruling queens in history, she controlled Egypt for two decades.

Her mortuary shrine remains one of the most elegant works on the Nile. Where the broad, dead-end valley of Deir el Bahri stops, the temple snuggles against a cliff 948 feet high. If Hatshepsut's architect had been a man of mediocre talent, the upward sweep of rough rock would have overpowered his structure. But the brilliant builder named Senmut placed the temple on two wide, columned terraces, putting width in perfect balance with the precipice above.

I found the terraces in good condition. In time to come, the temple, too, might rise again. Here, and all over Egypt, ruins grow less ruined by the year as archeologists piece together shattered stones.

From Deir el Bahri, I went to see paintings in tombs of ancient noblemen and queens. Along the dusty paths, merchants sat cross-legged under umbrellas.

"Cola, dear mister?" offered one, snapping open a bottle. Guides called dragomans competed for trade until I chose one and the rest went back to their shade.

Art vendors approached me, as they often did in Luxor, to offer me a fragment of antiquity. Stealthily, they opened a fold of their robes to show a chunk of fresco or a statue, and whispered, "Ten pounds?"

Ramadan Saad, Inspector of Antiquities at Luxor and a member of the National Geographic Society, had warned me that 95 percent of these objects are false, made by villagers of the area.

I went on to the cramped tombs. There I

Brand-new "antiquities" lure buyers along the visitors' route to the Valley of the Kings, west of the Nile. Villagers copy ancient relics and

FREELANCE PHOTOGRAPHERS GUILD (ABOVE); ROGER WOOD STUDIOS (LEFT); AND JOHANNA FARREN, NATIONAL GEOGRAPHIC STAFF

coat them with mud, making the pieces look like archeological finds.

Elegance in the desert, the temple of Hatshepsut marks Deir el Bahri, monument to a remarkable woman king. The stepmother, aunt, and co-regent of Thutmosis III, she assumed the throne, declared herself king, even wore the kilt and false beard of a Pharaoh at ceremonial occasions. Later Thutmosis regained power and sought to erase her name from shrine inscriptions.

Hathor, in her customary guise as a cow, licks a royal hand in this carved detail on a wall of her small chapel at Hatshepsut's temple at Deir el Bahri. Goddess of love, happiness, dance, and music, Hathor also guarded this part of the Theban necropolis.

felt the heat more keenly than in the desert sun. The guide beamed sunlight against the walls with a mirror. All around us the tomb came alive with color. Hundreds of ancient citizens acted out events that happened 3,000 years ago: the king's court at a royal festival, aristocrats visiting flowering gardens, workmen making mud bricks, ornate boats cruising up and down the Nile.

Neither guides nor vendors wait at the statues that Romans called the Colossi of Memnon. These two giants sit alone in a patch of farmland near the desert. Amenophis III, who began the temple at Luxor, stationed them here some 3,400 years ago to celebrate his glory.

At first they guarded a magnificent temple. An ancient inscription describes it: "... an eternal, everlasting fortress of... sandstone, embellished with gold throughout; its floor adorned with silver. . . ."

Erected when Egyptian wealth and artistry were at their height, the temple may have been everything these words imply—except eternal. Within two centuries, King Merneptah, with an irreverence common among Egyptian royalty, had stolen it piece by piece for his own mortuary shrine, leaving only the two stone colossi.

Looking southwest, I noticed earth embankments still visible among the crops. They mark the bounds of an artificial lake, wider than the Nile, that once rippled here. Beyond it stood the palace of Amenophis.

Royal residences, unlike temples, were not built for eternity. Here, as on other palace sites, archeologists find only crumbled rows of mud brick. But they have done a thorough job with these, salvaging frescoes that hint of dazzling decorations, and tracing buildings and courtyards that may have covered 80 acres. Local villagers gave the site its name, Malkata—Place Where Things Are Picked Up.

Malkata may have been the boyhood home of a Pharaoh insignificant in his own time but a sensation in ours. Born in an era of eminent kings, he did not distinguish himself in life. He did not have time; he died before he was 21 years old. But of all the royal tombs in the Valley of the Kings, only his survived unplundered. In 1922, English archeologist Howard Carter found the king's funeral treasure, and all the world came to know of King Tutankhamun.

His crypt held a fabulous hoard of wealth. Everything there—from the body in its golden coffins to clothing, jewels, and a glittering throne—showed a monarch ready for a rich afterlife.

But what of his life on earth? The tomb told little of that. Experts have spent decades gathering shards of evidence and piecing them together with informed theories. From their scholarly detective work comes a plausible story of Tutankhamun's brief stay in the world of the living.

The Colossi of Memnon, as the Romans named them, are 64-foot figures of Amenophis III. They mark the site of the vanished temple he "fashioned to last forever." Water from the Nile brought inland by canal laps at their bases.

About the age of four, the royal heir would have started school, since Egyptians of high rank began their education young. Princes from conquered lands, wards of the state who would take Egyptian culture back to their own countries, studied in the palace with Tutankhamun and young Egyptian nobles.

To read and write, Tutankhamun and his classmates had to work with some 700 symbols. Many of them were obvious pictures: birds, snakes, faces, whole human figures in different poses for different meanings. Others were equally pictorial but less obvious: a long oval for mouth, a wiggling line for water.

Complications entered, however, when a picture did not necessarily mean what it showed. In Tutankhamun's time, perhaps only a hundred or so did—a picture of a bee, for example, meaning either bee or honey. The rest of the symbols could stand for sounds as well—an owl, for instance, meaning *m*, a goose signifying *sa*. Putting these together somewhat as we combine letters, the Egyptians could write almost anything they wished.

When he was only nine or ten years old, Prince Tutankhamun became monarch. It was a shaky nation the boy inherited. His elder brother had upset powerful priests and citizens as well with a sweeping ideological reform. Crowned as Amenophis IV, he had changed his name to Akhenaten, abolished Amun and more than a hundred other gods, moved his capital downriver, and tried to force his country's ancient culture into a new mold of his own making.

Valley of the Kings held secret tombs of Theban monarchs. One escaped thorough looting: that of

We do not know what happened to the heretic king. But a long inscription, composed for the great temple at Karnak, tells us what had happened to Egypt:

"Now when his majesty [Tutankhamun] appeared as king, the temples of the gods and goddesses from Elephantine to the Delta . . . had fallen into neglect; their temples had gone to ruin. . . .

"The land was upside-down, and as for the gods, they forsook this land. If soldiers were sent to Syria to extend the borders of Egypt, their efforts were in vain."

Tutankhamun, reigning under advisers, "took counsel with his heart" and undertook to placate the gods whose "hearts were angry in their bodies." He moved the capital back to Thebes, and he "made monuments for all the gods, fashioning their statues of fine-gold, restoring their shrines . . . providing them with perpetual gifts . . . and supplying their earthly provisions."

About 1340 B.C., King Tutankhamun died. He had ruled no more than ten years. Unlike most Pharaohs, he did not have a tomb ready for him. Workers in the Valley of the Kings had 70 days to get one ready, the time required to prepare the body for its "voyage of eternity."

As all Egypt mourned, the body went to skilled morticians. While they worked, priests recited prayers. Finally the embalmers wrapped the mummy in hundreds of yards of fine linen, and the priests chanted: "You live again, you live again forever, here you are young once more for ever."

The funeral began at the palace. Women of the harem wore pale blue tunics made to be torn and stained with dust, as a symbol of sorrow. At the mummy's feet, the widow

ELIOT ELISOFON (ABOVE) AND DAVID S. BOYER, NATIONAL GEOGRAPHIC STAFF

ıtankhamun, rectangular opening on valley floor.

Within the burial chamber, National Geographic Society officers Dr. Leonard Carmichael (left) and Dr. Thomas W. McKnew flank Ramadan M. Saad, Inspector of Antiquities at Luxor. Outermost coffin of King Tutankhamun lies before a mural of the god Osiris (left) receiving the young ruler.

recited words that called for her husband's rebirth. Priests raised the body, carrying it to a canopied sled drawn by red oxen. A long procession began.

Over the plain of western Thebes the funeral march crept forward, first by land, then by canal boats. Professional mourners wailed. Courtiers followed the Pharaoh with treasure for the afterworld. The procession halted at the king's mortuary temple to spend four days in ritual that would assure him new life. On the fifth day, the procession began again.

I followed its route from Malkata to the Valley of the Kings. The road skirts the eastern face of the mountain, past the temples I had already seen, until it winds into a narrow gorge. Leaving the river and the plain behind, a path now paved twists through clefts of rock into the dazzling world of the Western Desert. Then the gorge widens. Ringed in blinding tan cliffs, the Valley of the Kings opens ahead.

Here, with offerings of blue flowers, the body of Tutankhamun was laid in its hastily finished tomb, while a cry of grief rang out: "I am thy wife, O great one—do not leave me!" At last the mourners departed, returning the valley to its silence.

How well did the secret valley protect the bodies entombed there? Not very well at all. In spite of all precautions thieves broke into most of the crypts, making off with the treasures, sometimes burning the mummies. Some ancient officials had a hand in the looting; even priests dabbled in theft.

Tutankhamun—his name as he spelled it in his cartouche (left), sign of royalty. Reading from the lower left, the quail and the two half-rounds spell *Tut;* next, the symbol of life is *Ankh;* the three elements at the top combine as *Amun*, god of Thebes, and thus take the position of honor in the cartouche. Tutankhamun came to the throne young; he ruled briefly; he died 3,300 years ago. He was indeed reborn—the purpose of his elaborate funeral and tomb—when archeologist Howard Carter discovered his crypt in 1922. It held a fabulous treasure nearly intact, the first such hoard recovered in Egypt. Plunderers had entered the tomb, Carter determined, and left its offerings in the jumble seen above as Carter found them. But the robbers had stolen little. Carved animal-shaped bed (at center, above) may have held the king's body for embalming; the gilded head (detail, left) in the shape of a hippopotamus represents Thoueris, goddess of birth. At right, Carter chips away sacred oils solidified between two of the Pharaoh's coffins. Fitted over the bandaged face of the mummy within, the superb portrait mask of beaten gold (above, right) showed the king protected by the vulture and the cobra, symbols of his twin realms, Upper and Lower Egypt.

COLOR PHOTOGRAPHS BY F. L. KENETT © GEORGE RAINBIRD LTD.

BLACK AND WHITE PHOTOGRAPHS COURTESY THE METROPOLITAN MUSEUM OF ART

ROGER WOOD STUDIOS

Grasping the rod of majesty and the flail of power, Tutankhamun rides a black panther in this statuette, one of four similar carvings found in his tomb. He wears the White Crown of Upper Egypt, adorned with the royal serpent.

Other priests, however, despising such blasphemy, frantically hustled mummies from one hiding place to another. Ramesses III was entombed four times, and an unfinished tomb at Deir el Bahri became the final ancient resting place for 35 bodies.

Right up to the present, western Thebes has provided all the thrills of a desert treasure island. Mr. Ramadan told me, "I think some of the villagers, living in huts built against ancient tombs, still hope to find antiquities. They use the tombs for storage or bedrooms. They work their fields in the daytime. At night they go home and dig.

"We inspect the tombs at intervals to make sure relics we know about haven't been tampered with. The last big tomb robbery in western Thebes happened in 1941. People got into 16 tombs and took plaster inscriptions to sell, but all of them were caught. Now we have many policemen to stop illegal trading in such things."

"Is there any chance of major new discoveries?" I asked.

"In the past ten years," he said, "we've identified about ten new sites, some temples but most of them tombs."

"Do you think you might find something more spectacular," I persisted, "like King Tutankhamun's tomb?"

"Possibly, yes," he answered. "Queen Hatshepsut has never been found. Some of the other Pharaohs are still missing. And no one has excavated thoroughly in an area we call the Western Valley, a second valley of kings. Yes, there's always the possibility of anything here."

In the Valley of the Kings, archeologists have found more than 60 tombs, all but Tutankhamun's despoiled. They recovered mummies of important kings, and valuable objects that early robbers had left behind. But by 1922, no one in modern times had seen a royal crypt with more than a fraction of its treasure intact.

Howard Carter had no reason to expect a bonanza on November 4 of that year, when he uncovered a rubble-strewn step below the tomb of Ramesses VI. But the 49-year-old archeologist considered even a new step a triumph. His colleagues had been tearing up the area for more than a century; only ten years before, one of them

Emblem of Hathor, a cow's head shows exacting workmanship; black glass outlines eyes of limestone and obsidian. Anubis (below), the canine "lord of the necropolis," keeps an alert vigil over the king he must lead to the other world.

F. L. KENETT © GEORGE RAINBIRD LTD.

Pharaoh's throne went with him into the afterlife, blazing with gold, silver, semiprecious stones, and glass. Small pendant at right depicts the king's predecessor and presumed father, Amenophis III.

Symbol of rebirth, a gosling breaks free of its egg, as the king would burst the shell of death. The nest covers an alabaster unguent jar. Mirror case at right center takes the form of the ankh, Egyptian sign of life. A reflector of polished metal once fitted inside the case.

All-seeing eye of Horus stares from one of the grave's finest jewels. Translucent quartz scarab forms the body of a bird with wings spread. Darkened moon holds image of Tutankhamun (center) escorted by Thoth (left) and Horus.

had written, "I fear that the valley... is now exhausted."

Clearing that step, and then 15 more below it, Carter saw that someone had preceded him. A doorway at the bottom, blocked with stones, had been broken, though plastered shut again. Near the entrance, Carter found seals of Tutankhamun. He rushed a cable to Highclere Castle in England, home of his wealthy patron, Lord Carnarvon.

The Earl reached Luxor on November 23. Two days later, in the Valley of the Kings, Carnarvon and Carter watched workmen hack the door away. Removing rubble from the tunnel beyond took four days longer. Then the workmen cut into a second blocked door. Carter peered through the first small hole.

"As my eyes grew accustomed to the light," he related, "details of the room within emerged slowly... strange animals, statues, and gold—everywhere the glint of gold."

Robbers had indeed broken into the four-room stronghold, perhaps only a few years after Tutankhamun's death. But inlaid chests, gilded chariots, weapons, trumpets, and clothing remained, with jewels, riding gloves, pieces of beef and other food, and a throne plated with silver and gold. It took Carter six years to remove, record, and restore the treasure—more than 2,000 items.

Getting to the mummy itself was like opening a nest of Chinese boxes. In the northwest corner, the burial chamber, Carter found a gilded wooden structure, a shrine sixteen feet long, nine feet high. He swung open its wide double doors. A smaller shrine glittered inside, tented with a linen veil. Inside this, he found a third box; then another. The last contained a superbly sculptured stone sarcophagus.

Carter lifted the rough granite lid away. Within linen wrappings, he found a wooden coffin carved in the image of the king and gilded, fitted with silver handles. Opening this, he found garlands of leaves and blue lotus flowers spread over another gilded case. Inside lay the eighth and final container—a coffin of solid gold that weighed more than a ton.

Today, Cairo's Museum of Egyptian Antiquities guards the treasure. But I did not find an empty tomb. Descending deep into the burial chamber, I joined an eerie company of gods and mortals painted larger than life on the yellow wall ahead. At their feet, a huge sarcophagus yawns at the rock ceiling. The body of the young king lies inside, waiting for eternity within a shining coffin. Serene and rather weary, the golden face of Tutankhamun stares upward.

Life-size statue, a black and gilt image of Tutankhamun himself carrying mace and rod stood at door of the burial chamber. Skin of black, color of rebirth, identifies him with Osiris, king of the dead. Kilt bears the words, "The Good God of whom one [can] be proud...."

Loving concern for the king shows on the face of the goddess Selkit, who guards a chest containing jars that hold his viscera. Three other goddesses protected the other sides.

11

JOURNEY INTO TIME

THE ROAD TO CAIRO is as long as you make it. An efficient driver, mapping a careful course, could go from Luxor to the capital in 410 miles. I did not expect to do nearly as well. Roads scribble over the wide and fertile banks, and every tantalizing fork taken puts the destination a few miles farther away. A determined curiosity, other travelers told me, can more than double the distance.

Goddard's party, with kayaks, arms toughened by paddling, and unlimited time, pushed north on the Nile. But I found downstream navigation, early in the spring, nearly paralyzed. Low water level left the current weak. Hot, sandy winds of the season howled the other way. Few boatmen cared to tack against miles of galloping whitecaps if they could wait for better sailing weather. So I filled a basket with fruit, a cornbread called *bettaw,* and roasted pigeons stuffed with corn, and set out overland.

The first compelling detour lies about 40 miles from Luxor, at the town of Qena. Feluccas packed with people and animals glide across the river here, and donkeys waiting on the western bank carry visitors to the temple of Dandara. Many travelers come to see a likeness of Cleopatra, sculptured into one wall with the son she bore to Julius Caesar. "She's not very pretty," a lady from Minnesota whispered to me. But it is probably inferior artistry, rather than the queen herself, that accounts for her lack of beauty. The temple, only 20 centuries old, arose in the waning years of Egyptian culture.

A humbler form of art fared better in the Qena region. In the days of the Pharaohs, people along this last great loop in the river evolved a plump and graceful design for one of Egypt's most vital utensils—the water jug. Ever since, their descendants have sustained the industry.

In the soft shade of palm trees, women mix brownish-gray clay with water and chaff. Most of them use their feet to knead the thick paste. The mixture goes to little huts made of mud brick and pottery fragments where men pump shaping wheels, also with their feet. They form a new pot between their fingers every two minutes. All around, pitchers dry in the sun—about four hours in summer, eight in winter.

At a village named El Ballâs, on the west bank, the thick black smoke of dried cornstalks smears the air over baking kilns. And along the river, boats sail away in both directions under ten-foot mounds of pottery.

"I have seen all of the suns men can remember .... Close to the Nile I watch over the plateau of Gîza," says the Great Sphinx, painted with lights during a historical dramatization held on the desert. An Egyptian king excavated the human-headed lion from a shroud of sand 34 centuries ago. At that time the limestone beast was already 1,100 years old.

NATIONAL GEOGRAPHIC PHOTOGRAPHER WINFIELD PARKS

Age-old industry: Potters shape jars of many sizes by hand. Using a foot-powered wheel they can fashion a jar every two minutes. Early Egyptians made pottery from clay found in Qena, where the craft still thrives.

Pattern of pots, called *ballas,* looms behind a worker in Qena. This Egyptian town north of Luxor makes several million clay jars yearly.

Voluminous robes veil women of Nag 'Hammâdi who watch over a cluster of water jars. *Naggars* like the two floating by will bear the jugs down the Nile to markets in Cairo and Alexandria. Shapes unchanged since Biblical days distinguish the earthenware.

This can be like carrying a cargo of eggs. As Egypt's main highway, the Nile often feels the pinch of traffic jams. The Johnsons encountered one when the *Yankee* reached a drawbridge at Nag 'Hammâdi, 30 miles north of Qena. As they waited for the span to open, Mrs. Johnson reported, "a file of feluccas with immense loads of straw and cane went scudding upriver, looking like squared haystacks with sails.

"Plainly, the helmsman at the stern was blind to what lay ahead, so each captain shouted orders from atop the haystack.

"*Yankee* hustled up behind the last two 'stacks' and found them fighting to gain priority. Both crews now stood on top of the straw, shrieking insults. Then came the collision, an anticlimax, soft and quiet, haystack to haystack. That seemed to settle something. As the feluccas parted, the . . . winner streaked for the . . . opening."

Suddenly, to everyone's amazement, the span began to close. The first boat and then the second swept helplessly against it. Puzzling over the bridge tender's action, the Johnsons towed the crippled feluccas to safety before making their own way along the river.

Ancient records show that nautical squabbles like this are nothing new on the Nile. Artists of pharaonic times "invariably" pictured boatmen fighting, one scholar points out. In a scene sculptured 4,300 years ago, crewmen attack each other with

Patchwork of cultivated squares soaks in the Nile's silt-laden floodwater. "They tremble that behold the Nile in full flood," wrote an ancient poet of the annual inundation. "The fields laugh and the river-banks are overflowed. The visage of men is bright, and the heart of the gods rejoiceth."

ELIOT ELISOFON

World's oldest free-standing stone structure, the Step Pyramid, built at Saqqâra about 2650 B.C.

poles, shouting the Old Kingdom equivalent of "Slosh him!"

Most roads between Nag 'Hammâdi and Cairo run along the western bank. The land here, lower and easier to irrigate, holds most of the people as well. But the roads rarely see traffic jams. Often my driver aimed his car right down the middle, between files of donkeys, camel trains, and women with bundles on their heads.

Near the town of El Balyana, the driver left the river road and turned directly inland. Another temple? More tombs? Both, I learned, and quite special ones at that, for we stopped at a spot called Abydos.

Five thousand years ago, this area was the burial ground for a city known as Thinis, home of Egypt's first historic kings. They ruled from Memphis, some 300 miles north. But during the first two dynasties they built mausoleums in the wild, silent hills of Abydos, structures that we call mastabas because they resemble rectangular Arab benches of that name. An architectural version of prehistoric burial mounds, mastabas often grew to huge proportions, with rooms for both bodies and storage.

Today, only rubble piles mark the tombs of Aha, Djer, and other superlatively ancient kings. Among them lies a chamber, part of a tomb built for a ruler named Khasekhemui, that archeologists say is one of the oldest stone constructions in the world.

Legend gave Osiris, king of the dead, a grave at this sacred city, and rulers raised grand buildings nearby until the nation's 30 dynasties came to an end.

One of the most beautiful temples on the Nile stands among the ruins here. Pharaoh Sethos I commanded it into being almost 3,300 years ago, a magnificent monument including two great columned halls and sanctuary rooms for seven gods. Egyptian art was only beginning its slow decline then, and reliefs chipped into the limestone walls rank among the finest in the country.

TOR EIGELAND, BLACK STAR (ABOVE) AND ROGER WOOD STUDIOS

ses 200 feet above the palm-fringed desert.

Builder of Egypt's first pyramid: King Djoser, ruler in the IIId Dynasty, changed the custom of burying kings in rectangular tombs called mastabas. When he ordered his funerary chamber, his favorite official, Imhotep, invented the step pyramid. Later Pharaohs streamlined the design into the true pyramid form.

In basic form, they appear no different from other human figures that Egyptians fashioned on flat surfaces. Deities and dignitaries stand with feet pointed along the wall, bodies swiveled toward the viewer, faces in profile—a pose that would be very difficult to hold. But this was the classic stance in art, passed down from earliest times. Outstanding works like these differ not in form, but in workmanship and grace. At Abydos, artists labored with nothing short of affection, modeling flesh and long, tight gowns with hundreds of precise chisel strokes.

The banks of the Nile turn drowsy when midday heat floods the valley. Dozing for moments, then waking again, I looked out on a land, though strange, at once familiar. To either side lay the world of children's tales I remembered—the valley always green where sun shines forever, walled in perfect isolation by starkly gleaming cliffs.

Few people stroll along the road at this time of day, and shops close about one o'clock. At times, the only thing moving is the river, pouring north like liquid chrome. Then boats come into sight, making little wrinkles in the water with their bows and sliding out of view without a sound.

About four, the road comes to life again. Children wearing hardly more than birthday bronze swoop down mudslides into the irrigation canals. Just outside a village, a golden blizzard blows from the communal *gurn*, or threshing square, as women fork wheat into the wind. And a car creeps down a street of dusty, cluttered shops that will be busy until eight o'clock at night.

Smaller villages stand back from the road, clusters of ten or fifteen huts in a grove of palms. Stopping near one, I followed a dike across the fields and scuffed into a spiderweb of lanes. As long as even the local wise man could remember, no foreigner had

Abode of the dead, domed tombs stretch along the Nile beneath stark cliffs at Zâwyet el Amwât.

walked here before. The *'umda,* or headman, greeted me with the smiling and unfailing hospitality of Egypt.

When the 'umda handed me a glass of fiercely black boiled tea, I noticed a tattoo on his hand—a large blue pattern, to ward off the malice of evil spirits. Few treat supernatural forces lightly; some believe they cause sickness and death. Youngsters who chattered along behind me wore blue beads around their necks to protect them from the evil eye.

Many communities have a sorcerer, preferably a Coptic Christian. He combats the evil eye, and works against the power of jinns, or spirits, as well. If sorcery fails and evil strikes, people may turn to the local *mizayyen,* a barber who pulls teeth, treats wounds, gives vaccinations, and serves as coroner if all remedies fail.

In many villages, I found signs of change mixed with ways of the past. Television sets—battery-powered where electricity has not yet arrived—brought the world to public squares. On a single night, I watched a government debate, a religious drama, and a wild-west film with whips of Arabic across the bottom.

ELIOT ELISOFON

odern Islamic burial ground, it adjoins one dating from the days of the earliest dynasties.

If a town is lucky, it may have a two-story social center as well—an innovation that has brought farm advisors, recreation directors, and medical teams to the countryside since 1936.

Some villages have not been lucky yet, since Cairo has only so much money for such amenities. Yet mobile health units roll in from provincial capitals every so often. Well-drillers have, in recent years, bored down through Nile silt to bring up clear, clean water. And superstitions tend to pale in the light of education as primary schools come to one village after another.

In days past, rural people looked upon central government as an alien force. Often the view was valid. Egypt saw 40 years of formal British occupation. Before that, it lived under Turkish rule and French; under beys who came from as far away as eastern Europe; under Arab caliphs and Byzantine emperors; under Romans, Greek Ptolemies, and Persian conquerors who began the chain of foreign-descended rulers. When army officers exiled King Farouk, whose family originated in Albania, they severed the chain, which by then reached back into history more than two millenniums.

Since the revolution in 1952, the government has stressed a policy of "Egyptianization," with one eye on the proud pharaonic past and the other on a future newly full of hope.

Halfway between Luxor and Cairo, I found the ruins of an ancient hope that failed, a great city that rose and fell in a single generation. Modern maps call the place Tell el 'Amârna. But 3,300 years ago, Egyptians knew the city as Akhetaten, a brand new capital built for the Pharaoh from Thebes who was changing everything.

Amenophis IV may have been a bold politician, a courageous idealist, or a negligent king. Modern opinions vary. In his extraordinary reign, he defied the most sacred traditions of the Nile nation.

Perhaps his predecessor, Amenophis III, had sown the seeds of this royal rebellion years before, when he opposed tradition and powerful priests of Amun to make a commoner his queen. Certainly the young Pharaoh felt the effects of this. As he took the throne, Queen Tiye and perhaps Amenophis III still lived; the rift between throne and temple remained to hinder him.

The new king acted decisively. He abolished the great god Amun altogether, and condemned scores of lesser deities as well. In their place, he proclaimed only one god —Aten, the sun's disk.

He changed his name—which meant "Amun is satisfied"—to Akhenaten, "it is well with Aten." He changed his capital, sailing 240 miles north of Thebes to Akhetaten—"the Horizon of Aten." In the fine new city, the royal family maintained at least three palaces, and some of the poorest workmen had at least two rooms in their homes. All new and dazzling white, Akhetaten followed the bank for five miles.

Its artists developed a revolutionary style, showing the Pharaoh and his family as

Sure-footed sailor clings to the yard of his craft as he furls the large sail. To catch the slightest whisper of air the long spar may stretch the mainsail 130 feet aloft.

Casting a web of cord as did his forefathers centuries ago, an Egyptian tries to net a school of fish in the Nile. For millenniums civilizations of parched Egypt have drawn life from the river. "It flows through old hushed Egypt and its sands," wrote poet Leigh Hunt, "Like some grave mighty thought threading a dream."

human beings, rather than stylized gods. The Pharaoh himself, it appears, was preoccupied with praise to the beneficent Aten. He neglected his crumbling empire on the eastern Mediterranean shore. He seems not to have noticed unrest at home.

The Horizon of Aten lasted less than a generation. The Pharaoh vanished from history, no one knows how. His god and his city were abandoned. Later, the child monarch Tutankhamun "appeared as king . . . seeking what would be beneficial to his father Amun."

I found the royal dream completely ruined: empty tombs in the hills and a desert full of pillar stumps.

Moving north on inland roads, a traveler follows a legend. Baḥr Yûsef, people call it, one of Egypt's longest irrigation canals. Villagers still tell of a man named Yûsef, official of an ancient king, and how he fashioned its 161 very crooked miles within 70 days. But today authorities believe the waterway is natural over most of its length, possibly deepened to serve the Pharaohs.

Wiggling north, the channel suddenly

ELLIOTT ERWITT, MAGNUM (BELOW) AND GILBERT M. GROSVENOR, NATIONAL GEOGRAPHIC STAFF

veers into the Western Desert. One road turns the same way, following a slender green stem of fertile land to a vast leaf-shaped oasis. This is the Faiyûm—656 square miles of rich black earth supporting some 900,000 people.

A LAND OF WINES, roses, and palm groves surrounded by the desert, the Faiyûm is one of Egypt's loveliest farmlands. More olive trees grow here than anywhere else in the country. All around, oranges, lemons, and mandarins hang like little bright lanterns.

On the northern edge, a large lake lures ducks and pink flamingos here to build their nests. And pigeons—Egyptians keep them almost everywhere, but lofts in the Faiyûm mean big business, yielding up to six tons of fertilizer a year. Every evening, 20,000 birds may swoop toward a single rookery, a fortlike tower 30 feet tall.

When Herodotus stopped on the lakeshore, about 450 B.C., he found people who worshiped the crocodile. "They adorn his ears with ear-rings of molten stone or gold," he wrote, "and put bracelets on his fore-paws, . . . and, . . . they embalm him . . . and bury him in a sacred repository."

From the Faiyûm, Herodotus saw pyramids, too. So did I. For the next 60 miles the grandest tombs of Egypt spike the edge of the desert, leading all the way to Cairo.

Archeologists have found more than 70 pyramids in Egypt, some unfinished, many heaps of rubble now. Others, both large and insignificant, may lie undiscovered. The pyramid form remained a part of Egyptian architecture until Roman times. But the oldest, grandest pyramids belonged to Memphis, first capital of a united Egypt.

The city came into being about 3100 B.C., when King Menes built his fortress there. It remained important through all the days of ancient Egypt.

Yet, of the world's great cities of antiquity, few have been so absolutely wiped out. Ruins—miles of ruins—were trundled off to Cairo for centuries, providing one Arab caliph after another with prefabricated building stone. I found nothing more than an immense hollow here and there, a few mounds, a fine sphinx of alabaster, and a statue in a grove of palms.

But walking westward toward the land of the dead, I saw the same architectural sky-

Remnant of splendor, alabaster sphinx overshadow

line that overlooked the streets of Memphis 4,500 years ago. The first pyramid I came to, near the village of Saqqâra, is the very first one ever built.

A work of high genius, it honors a king who would not make up his mind. The genius was Imhotep, Vizier, Chief Carpenter, Chief Sculptor, Overseer of Works of Upper and Lower Egypt, and several other things—an important man indeed. The king was Djoser, who may have founded the IIId Dynasty when he came to the throne about 2686 B.C.

At first, the king's provision for afterlife was nothing special—a mud-brick mastaba near Abydos. Later, he decided to build a burial vault near his capital. Imhotep began the tomb at Saqqâra.

First he ordered a shaft hacked 92 feet into the desert's rock floor, with a crypt at

TOR EIGELAND, BLACK STAR

passing villagers. It survives at the site of the ancient city of Memphis, first capital of a united Egypt.

the bottom. Then he commanded a mastaba built over it. The building that went up was a new kind of structure—revolutionary, in fact. It became the first square tomb, about 207 feet along each side. More important, the building was the first in Egypt made entirely of stone.

Djoser must have been pleased with the massive box. He decided his family should be buried under it too. Imhotep extended the tomb.

Imhotep seems a restless genius, with a monarch of the same disposition, for they did not stop here. Once again they enlarged the mastaba—so they could build three more on top of it. The building soared in tall steps—Egypt's first pyramid.

But it was not finished. Imhotep expanded the whole structure—enormously—adding two more steps and covering everything with smooth white stone. Around the massive monument, he built courtyards, a temple, halls, chapels, and more than a mile of splendid stone walls enclosing them all.

From the ruins of Djoser's burial city, I saw other massive piles of stone—later refinements, not stepped, but in the true pyramid shape. The age of the grandest pyramids endured until the end of the VIth Dynasty, about 400 years after Djoser died.

But the IVth Dynasty produced the greatest pyramid of all, the tomb of King Cheops (Khufu) near the town of El Gîza. From a distance, it looked perfectly familiar, a giant reproduction of a hundred postcards I had seen. But as I walked around it one hot afternoon, I felt the postcards had failed to catch the spirit of growing thirst, frying pavement, and a stroll that seemed endless. Memorized facts helped to put the edifice into proportion: It soars as high as a 40-story building; the 13 acres under its base would hold nine football games at once; a larger stone structure has never been erected in all the history of man.

Yet the foundation lies only one-half inch away from perfect level. And originally the four sides matched in length within eight inches.

According to tradition, a ninth-century treasure hunter, Egypt's Caliph Mamun, hacked the passage I followed to the pyramid's interior. This led to the ancient, original shaft, a hot, steep tunnel so cramped that people fold up like jackknives to get through it. "Mind your head," I heard a guide advising from somewhere far away.

Unfolding in a lofty corridor called the Grand Gallery, I found wooden treads leading upward, fluorescent tubes lighting

Famed triumvirate of Gîza pyramids honors, from left, Kings Mycerinus, Chephren, and Cheops

the way. Cigarette smoke hung in little balloons for a moment before dissolving in dank, still air. And the heat here seemed little less than outside on the desert.

Then, strangely, a tunnel at the end of the Grand Gallery led to a breeze. Following marvelously fresh air through a passage once blocked by stone, I reached a room that Arabs called the King's Chamber. Here, in the heart of the pyramid, two shafts no wider than a man's arm lead through the walls, entryways, perhaps, for a dead king's spiritual being.

The chamber, 34½ feet long, holds nothing but a roughly hewn red granite sarcophagus. Its lid has vanished. One can only guess about treasures brought here for eternity. And the king who built the greatest pyramid of all? Of Cheops, not a pinch of dust remains.

usion to the contrary, Cheops' Great Pyramid rises two and one-half feet higher than the center tomb.

NATIONAL GEOGRAPHIC PHOTOGRAPHER WINFIELD PARKS

12

THE FERTILE WEDGE

GETTING UP at sunrise, I saw more than half of Egypt before breakfast. Half of Egypt? In a practical sense, yes, since Cairo and the Nile Delta hold this much of the country's cultivable land.

Minutes after my plane lifted off Cairo's desert airport, the part of Egypt called Lower Egypt began to take shape. We circled, gained altitude, and began to follow the river.

Directly below, a single stream licked through the sprawling capital, a city of sandcastles from this height. Then, 15 miles north, the river split in two. The Rosetta branch meanders more or less northwest. The Damietta channel twists away to the northeast. Both shoot a spray of canals for miles in every direction, for here, too, the Nile nourishes all life.

High in the region of geysering clouds, I saw most of Lower Egypt spreading below and understood instantly why Greeks called this area *delta.* Fertile land, like an open fan, nudges back the desert to east and west. Capital delta, the fourth letter in the Greek alphabet, forms the same sort of triangle. Among the world's largest deltas, this one reaches north for a hundred miles before coastal land breaks into salty lakes and sandspits. Along the sea, the span of green land spreads 180 miles wide.

Farmland here reminded me of a geometric game. A square of dark green bumps a rectangle of pale green; then comes medium green, with the next move into a patch of brown. Villages sprinkle the squares like pawns at the end of a chess match. Only larger cities seemed out of place: Damanhûr, Ṭanṭa, Zagazig, and several other cities sprawl like an invasion of mud-gray starfish.

Roads racing everywhere make the Nile's irrigated tassel look very busy and crowded. And so it is. Almost two-thirds of Egypt's people live in the deltaland, and 60 percent of the country's arable soil lies here. When my plane landed back at Cairo, I stepped out into the most crowded part of all.

The airport is crowded, jets whistling in from London, Capetown, New York, New Delhi. Hotels on the riverbank, often fully booked during winter months, look as busy as railroad stations. And the city itself? More than 3,500,000 citizens live in its web of twisted streets. Cairo is the largest metropolis in Africa, and the largest in the Arab world as well.

Cairenes represent nearly everybody. A dining-room hostess who takes orders in seven languages has genie eyes that hint of Oriental Jewish origin. Brown Nubians in silky white robes and scarlet sashes rustle

Pale mist of desert dust shrouds an old quarter of Cairo. Turkish-style Mosque of Muhammed Ali Pasha, a dynamic 19th-century ruler, looms in the distance from the city's commanding Citadel rock.

Threshold of the Delta, Cairo crowds the Nile. Irving Johnson's *Yankee,* with her candy-striped sail,

to the table with cracker-thin toast. A wine waiter delivering Vichy water has the features and accent of a Greek. And how could I fathom the ancestry of the taxi driver who insisted his cab was the best in Cairo?

"What you say? Ten pounds a day." His tan Latin features did not suggest any specific nation. "Eight pounds only for you, my friend." His smile belonged to all Egyptians, who say that other, more serious Middle Easterners have *dam ta 'il*—heavy blood. "O.K., dear sir. Half day, three pounds," about seven dollars.

Quite possibly his remote ancestors settled at the southern end of the city, where we stopped in a region called El Fusṭâṭ. According to some ancient writers, captives from Babylonia made their home here when Thebes ruled Egypt. However that may be, the car was parked only steps away from a fortress that Romans built on a site still known as Babylon.

The Roman bastions probably went up in the first century, when, according to tradition, St. Mark brought Christianity to Egypt. And two of them support El Mu'allaqa, "the Hanging Church," built about the fifth century and still serving Cairo's Coptic community.

The Reverend Father Shenouda Hanna showed me through his church, pointing out Byzantine icons, superb screens carved

N.G.S. PHOTOGRAPHER WINFIELD PARKS (ABOVE) AND TOR EIGELAND, BLACK STAR

passes business center (right) and Gezira Island.

in cedar and ebony, Coptic crosses inlaid in ivory.

And who are the Copts? Direct descendants of ancient Egyptians, Father Hanna told me. "Coptic people—there are more than six million today—have rarely intermarried with others," he explained.

Father Hanna opened a carved window screen to show me one of the Roman towers, still surrounded by its original moat. The Byzantine Empire, or Roman Empire

Needlelike Cairo Tower, a 630-foot-high observation pillar of neo-arabesque design, pierces the sky behind a vendor and her cartload of yellow beans, a popular snack eaten like popcorn.

NATIONAL GEOGRAPHIC PHOTOGRAPHERS WINFIELD PARKS (ABOVE AND BELOW RIGHT) AND JOSEPH J. SCHERSCHEL

Corniche of Cairo sprawls below the city's modern roofscape. Mute lions guard the entrance of El Tahrir Bridge (left). Alongside the esplanade, the river streams past the luxurious Nile Hilton (right). Visitors (below) tour the Egyptian Museum, a treasure house of antiquities.

First President of the United Arab Republic, Gamal Abdel Nasser waves to his countrymen.

of the East, lost this stronghold when another wave of foreigners cascaded up the Nile: the army of Omar, the caliph from Arabia. By A.D. 642, Egypt belonged to the swelling empire of Islam.

Cruising a few blocks north, the cab stopped in front of the Nile's oldest mosque, partly ruined but still in use, with new prayer mats spread between marble columns from ancient temples. An elderly attendant showed me around, patiently explaining everything in Arabic while I explained in gestures that I did not understand a word.

The driver translated for me as we left. According to tradition, the mosque proclaims the spot where the triumphant Arab general, ʿAmr ibn el-ʿĀs, pitched his tent. The first Moslem capital, El Fusṭâṭ, grew outward from it.

Then El Fusṭâṭ became Cairo?

"No sir. Don't be so hurry," the driver said soothingly. The city and its citizens are not so simple as that.

He knew a delightful story of Cairo's first day, July 6, 969. A group of Moslems called Fatimites had thundered east from what is now Tunisia and conquered Egypt for themselves. They strung ropes over bare earth to mark the limits of their new capital. Bells dangled from the cords so astrologers could signal the moment when the stars would favor the work.

Laborers waited to begin the walls. Astrologers calculated. Suddenly a crow perched on one of the ropes. Bells jingled and workmen leaped into action. So, while the planet *El Qâhir*—Mars—was ascendant, a bird founded *El Qâhira*—the Martian—as the Arabs named their city. Ever since, Cairo has been the capital of Egypt. But foreign invasions did not end with that.

Circling back toward the Nile, my taxi crept below the rock-top Citadel founded by Saladin. An Armenian Kurd brought up in Syria, he took over Egypt in 1168, and proved himself enlightened and just as its ruler. He won the admiration of both East and West as a chivalrous warrior in battles against Richard the Lionheart and crusading armies of Europe.

Behind the Citadel, in a desert valley, domes and minarets catch hot sun and tan shadows in an elegant lacework of sculpture. These are mosque-tombs of the Mamelukes, fierce warriors who lived their youth as slaves and grew up to rule the land.

Once an elite guard for Cairo's Arab sultans, Mamelukes snatched Egypt for themselves. As generations went by, they bought boys from their own homelands near Black and Caspian Sea shores, training the youths to succeed them. Lives of the Mamelukes read like Oriental legends—tales of lavish wealth, harem intrigue, the sudden dagger-stroke. Their power meant oppression and poverty for Egypt. But for Cairo, it meant beauty: acres of delicate artistry in stone.

MY DRIVER STOPPED at a splendid mosque built for the Sultan Hasan. Six centuries of dust dulled the walls, but he ignored the stonework, pointing to a single dark shape wedged high above us: a cannonball. It belonged to Napoleon, he told me. The French general's invasion in 1798 began the ruin of Mameluke power. And like so many invasions before, it brought fresh culture and more new faces to Cairo.

Who else is a Cairene? Certainly people like a European aristocrat I met have stayed long enough to be called natives. Some years before Hitler took over his homeland, he was disapproving of the Nazis over cakes at Groppi's cafe not far from the riverbank.

His fashionable expatriate group has dwindled. Its members have been trickling away ever since King Farouk vacated his palaces in 1952 and gaiety gave way to the serious business of factories and more efficient farms. But the displaced aristocrat continues to live in his drawing room with a fountain, because no other place would seem like home.

Perhaps Arab invaders of long ago tried to recreate the desert homes they left behind when they put their city on the arid bottom corner of the lush Delta. Almost everywhere I went in Cairo, I found the desert present.

A foreigner does not notice it immediately. The Nile paints a cool blue stripe past bright new waterside buildings, and trees flare along each bank like green torches. In Midan El Tahrir—Liberation Square—a fountain flashes into a circular pool and workers doze away their lunchtime on geometric patches of grass.

Yet, following pathways through the square, I found puffs of powdery earth tagging along behind my shoes. In front

Bustling bazaar: a shopkeeper bargains with a family over a cerise dress. North of the Citadel in Cairo a maze of markets displays silks and brocades, pots and pans, ivory and jewels.

Fashioning a star-shaped lantern, a coppersmith practices his craft in the bazaar district named Khaan el-Khaliili. He will deftly fit bits of glass into the arabesque lamp. Trays of intricate design lean next to the old artisan.

Nail polish and notions: In a shop open to a crowded street in the old bazaar area of Cairo, a woman extends her fingers for the shopkeeper to paint her nails red. Strands of beads, small plastic handbags, and lace-trimmed finery festoon the market stall.

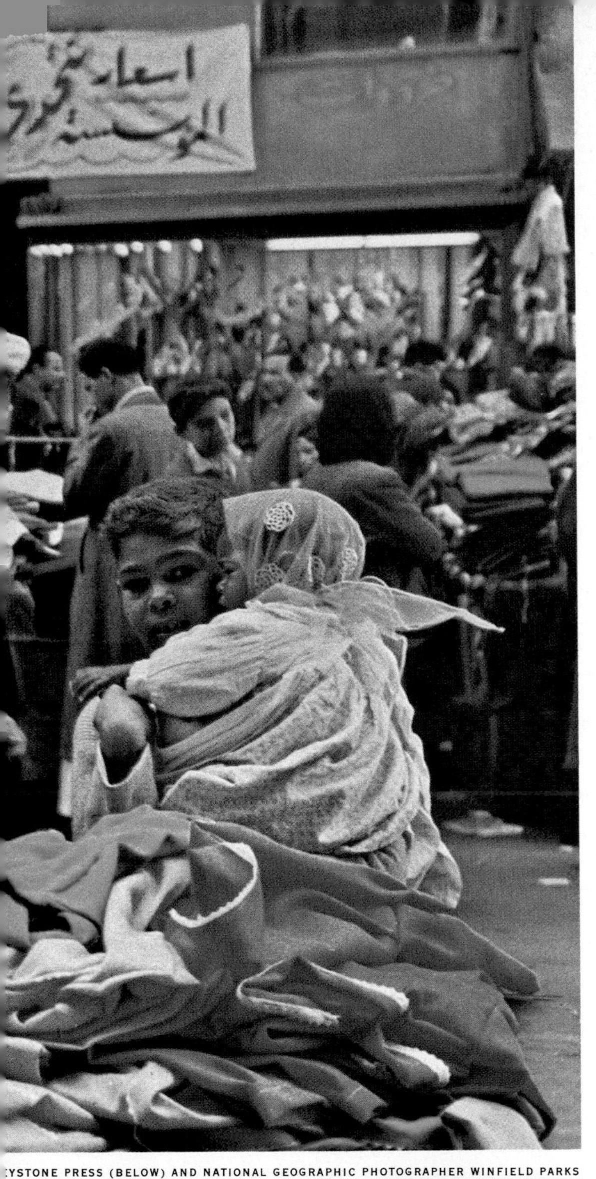

YSTONE PRESS (BELOW) AND NATIONAL GEOGRAPHIC PHOTOGRAPHER WINFIELD PARKS

of grand hotels, liveried Nubians spruced up the walls with feather dusters. In business districts, sidewalks of red and ivory mosaic would have looked like roads to a holiday, but a film of desert made their patterns barely noticeable.

Bad weather in Cairo does not mean rain. That comes only four or five times a year, and always with the springlike cool of winter. Summer heat can be hard to bear, but I found it no worse than August in Wisconsin. A day in Cairo goes bad only when winds arrive, shrouding the city in luminous dust.

But a windy day has beauty of its own; then the city turns vague as a vision in a pearl. One day as dust spirals spun in the desert hills, I watched the transformation from a new concrete tower on Gezira Island. Ordering lunch in a slowly revolving glass-walled restaurant near the 630-foot summit, I had a magic-carpet view over a fairy tale.

Sand-colored office buildings faded in tan air, no longer dominating domes and minarets of older times. Kites, birds always skimming Cairo's rooftops, swished past like black boomerangs, but nothing else was clear.

With an ounce of imagination, I found the Cairo of Saladin, who rode through the streets with a chain-mailed army. Where now boatmen lowered masts to glide under traffic bridges, Mamelukes had drifted on pleasure barges, puffing jeweled water-pipes. Where the Turkish-style mosque of Muhammed Ali Pasha soared from the Citadel rock, the pasha himself invited the Mamelukes he defeated to a friendly ceremony. Some 500 of the gorgeous warriors arrived in yellow turbans, red pantaloons, and pointed slippers. And as they rode in procession that day in 1811, Muhammed Ali's men, the legend says, butchered all but one, who spurred his horse off the Citadel walls and survived.

The wind fades after a couple of hours. So does old Cairo. Gezira Island, no longer a pleasure garden for beys, holds a racecourse and modern apartments. Tourists have replaced flamboyant armies in the Citadel. And busy streets below are full of middle-class businessmen more interested in politics than pashas.

I entered their world—a new world for Egypt—by car, racing south along the Nile.

Students meet in Oriental Hall at American University in Cairo. Nearly 1,000 undergraduates from 45 countries attend daytime classes at the midtown school; organization follows that of liberal arts colleges in the United States. Three larger universities—Al Azhar, Ain Shams, and the University of Cairo—also make their home in Greater Cairo. The oldest, Al Azhar, grew around a tenth-century mosque to become the world's leading center of Islamic education. The largest, Cairo University, enrolls 61,000 students.

Eyes shaded against furnace heat and glare, a student conducts an experiment to find a new laser crystal material at American University. The college has a solid-state science research program at the graduate level. It also offers a degree in the teaching of English as a foreign language.

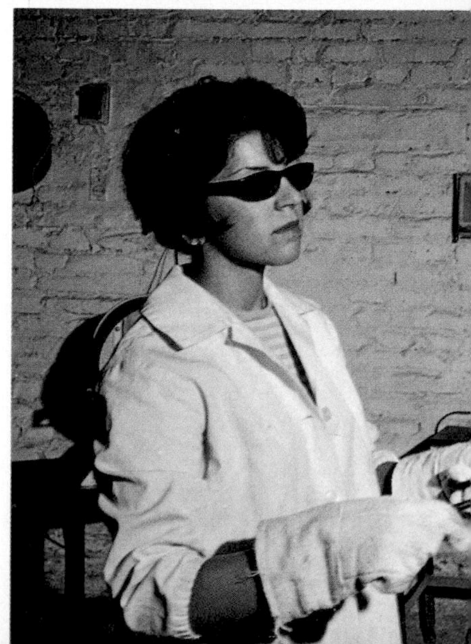

TOR EIGELAND, BLACK STAR

For miles, I found steelwork rushing up higher than minarets: apartments and hotels that bring quick returns to investors. Government housing developments spread far into desertland. And new factories testified to an astonishing drive to industrialize: Between 1952 and 1963, the country's factory output leaped 304 percent.

Nothing impresses a modern Egyptian more than industrial plants. He looks upon them with the tender affection that English men feel for Elizabethan cottages, and some he guards with machine guns. Along the southward road, I found farmers proud to see a factory churning out cement on the edge of their fields.

At the town of Helwân, a former spa for the wealthy, now an industrial suburb, I watched pilgrims of the new age staring in awe at the Egyptian Iron and Steel Company plant. Cotton from Egyptian fields supplies many of the country's production lines. Other plants turn sugar, fruits, minerals, and chemicals into products for the international marketplace.

One of the Arab world's most fascinating marketplaces twists through the heart of Cairo. It strays for miles, a crowded curl of narrow lanes full of incense smells and oily hints of flower attar. Many streets display simple goods: bolts of cotton; plastic toys; stiff, lacy vegetable fiber, called loofa, used for scrubbing the skin. But the section I returned to often and never saw completely, the suq of Khaan el-Khaliili, deals in everything from peanuts to pearls.

"A tooled bronze water-pipe for the gentleman?" merchants urged, sometimes pursuing me down the block. "Damascus brocades," others offered, or "a cane with a sword—real ebony. Ah, a gentleman of taste, I can see; my Persian carpets are dyed with old dyes—never fade—and the knots are ver-ry close together."

Under screened balconies, men in tiny family shops patiently hammer thousands of triangles into plates of copper. Boys fit bits of ivory into cedar platters. Little girls chip at gemstones creating lovely translucent scarabs.

Shopping for a pigeon-blood ruby, I always received coffee or mint tea before a merchant mentioned business. For a quarter-hour or so we would bargain—a common courtesy in suqs like this. I never found the stone I sought, but merchants

seemed satisfied with coffee and conversation. Inefficient? Perhaps. But delightful.

Sahran, an Arabic adjective, means "staying up long into the night." Many Cairenes do. Hours after nightfall, I found men talking politics in a sort of village-style sidewalk cafe called *baladī*. As late as 10 p.m., I could find a restaurant for mutton kabob, rice with pine kernels, and sherbet under rose syrup. Later still, glassed wagons creaked through the streets with stacks of plates and piles of spiced beans for sale.

When the very poor spread rush mats on the sidewalk for the night, hundreds of guards emerge to patrol the city. Turkish baths that seem never to close huff steam from their doorways. And how late, I wondered nightly, would Arabic music agonize out of loudspeakers all over Cairo?

"An experience in weird and irrational navigation," the Johnsons called their journey between Cairo and the sea. Low water barred them from the Nile itself, so the *Yankee* sailed the Beheira Canal, one of the navigation channels in the Delta. Bridges, usually opening only at night, "proved nightmares, blocking traffic for hours. When a bridge finally opened, the effect was of dynamite on a log jam, but with a difference: As the span lifted, everything

TOR EIGELAND, BLACK STAR

Throng of spectators follows a soccer game in the Cairo Stadium, one of the largest in the Middle East. The two-tiered oval can hold as many as 100,000 spectators. Opened in 1960, it forms the keystone structure of a multimillion-dollar sports complex that sprawls between Cairo and the northeastern suburb of Heliopolis. Because the dry, warm climate of Egypt encourages open-air sports, tennis, golf, swimming, yachting, riding, and fishing clubs abound in the capital. Basketball, boxing, and wrestling compete with football as the country's most popular sport. Racing of pure-blooded Arabian horses also draws large weekend crowds. Oarsmen in Cairo (below) skim a racing shell past a houseboat on a canal that branches off the Nile.

Five thousand years of Mediterranean civilization meet in ways and faces found along the timeless Egyptian Nile. Rich farmland deposited by floods of the past yields a year-round bounty, often under tools, techniques, and irrigation devices familiar to the Pharaohs. Arabic heritage and the faith of Islam, both with roots in the seventh century, guide national life, combining steadily with modern international ideas. Faces of Egypt sometimes resemble gods and mortals portrayed in stone on ancient temple walls. Others evolved as a rich blend of peoples passed through Nile history: Egyptians, Greeks, and Romans of antiquity, and later settlers who came from nearby lands in Asia and Europe.

TOP ROW, SECOND, THIRD, SIXTH PHOTOGRAPHS N.G.S. PHOTOGRAPHER WINFIELD PARKS; SECOND ROW, THIRD PHOTOGRAPH WINFIELD PARKS, FOURTH ROGER WOOD STUDIOS; ALL OTHERS TOR EIGELAND, BLACK STAR

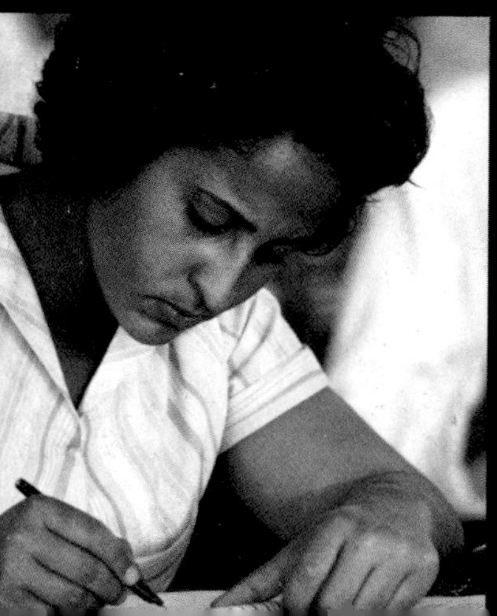

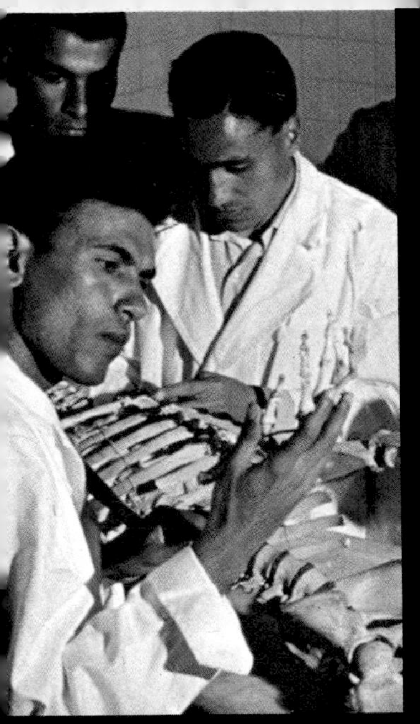

TOR EIGELAND, BLACK STAR

Classic costumes: A Bedouin woman wearing the desert headcloth called *tarha* balances a water jar. A Delta merchant robed in a *galabia* shoulders a pillar of baskets. "Egyptian boys and many men wear striped cotton suits identical to our pajamas," says the author.

rushed through—to meet headlong with a jam coming the other way. In the blackness . . . the result was bedlam." Their 200-mile journey lasted a week.

Setting out by road, I found the sea less than half a day away. The Nile-side corniche sweeps northward from the city, lined with flame trees all the way. A fine divided highway takes over, lancing into flat, green land.

Some of the most productive farmland in the world, the Delta seems an agricultural fantasy. Growing season can be any season. Water is always available, though the lilac sky is rainless most of the year.

Without the Nile, desert would reclaim this land. But Nile-dwellers themselves are fully as responsible for the Delta's luxuriance. They have used the river and its silt as raw material, piling up dikes and flooding canals to maintain the area as a vast artificial garden. Running away into buttery sunshine, the lacework of canals suggests a Mediterranean Holland.

Barrages—low stone dams—hold the river level high so water can be portioned into irrigation channels through the year. I came upon the first set of barrages just north of Cairo, where the Nile splits and wanders on in two main channels.

The first modern barrages, ordered in the 19th century by Muhammed Ali Pasha, look more like castles than dams, with moats, bastions, and turrets. They no longer hold back the river; newer walls streak across the streams a mile or so north. Instead, they are part of a park where I found city people picnicking and playing ball under tall shade trees. Children, conscious of schoolwork even on a holiday, stopped me several times to test their English: "What time is it now?" asked a boy with a watch of his own; "How are you? Are you English? You are welcome."

Irrigation water courses away into the Delta's share of a nationwide canal network some 54,000 miles long. Many channels are narrow enough for a donkey to hop. Others slip between high dikes like major rivers, and often I saw sails rising strangely in a grove of palms.

In every village I passed, dusty market streets showed the Delta's bounty: melons by the pile, reed mats full of turnips and leeks, baskets of tomatoes, mangoes, and apricots. Gardens in the countryside foamed with flowers, shedding the scent of jasmine and lilies. Lotus flowers, a favorite of ancient Egyptians, grow only in the Delta. Roses, a favorite of Arabs, develop an aroma as heady as wine.

But more than food and flowers, Egypt wants cotton from the Nile's fertile wedge. Of all the country's earnings from abroad, more than 70 percent comes from cotton, some of the finest grown anywhere, with fibers up to 1¾ inches long.

When the Delta turns snowy with a new crop, the whole population has cotton on its mind. Women and children wade through a blizzard of bolls, plucking the

Vegetable vendor stops his cart below a window in Damanhûr to offer lettuce for a few piasters, equal to a few cents. Picture sign advertises "excellent ice cream"—strawberry and vanilla flavors especially recommended.

جيلاتي عبد المجيد الممتاز

TOR EIGELAND, BLACK STAR

"Like a Mediterranean Holland," noted the author in the lush meadowland of the Nile Delta (below). An irrigation canal carries Nile water past a thick carpet of ripened wheat. Slender date palms stretch above the fields. Each year the pipestem trees yield the most abundant fruit

mature fluff from the plants. Men sit in street cafes with buyers from Alexandria, sipping sweet black coffee and hailing this crop as the best in many years, surely worth the highest prices. In canal-side cities like Damanhûr, cotton bales tumble off the wharves and lint-covered barges slide away as white as wedding cakes.

Cotton cash makes a market like a festival. Fellahin invade the towns, buying clothing, furniture, pots and pans. Young couples outfit their future homes, for this is the season for marriage as well. Storytellers come to town, hoping to revive their fading art for a few days. And, if the town does not have a cinema, one will arrive in pieces on the back of a truck.

In the Delta's northland, towns thin out. Fewer minarets, palms, and smokestacks break the flat horizon. Marsh grass appears along the road. The air turns cool and wafts the smell of seaweed over lowland swamps. The terrain of Egypt is disintegrating.

Four great gray lakes blotch the Delta's coast, slender sandspits walling them from the sea. The few Egyptians I saw here looked more like Venetians, poling little boats through the reeds. Between the lakes, miles of dunes rise above a final fringe of palms. Just over them lies the sea.

From the town of Dumyât in the eastern Delta or from Rashîd in the west, a traveler can follow the Nile to its end. I chose Rashîd and traced a general path along the Nile's Rosetta branch, where John Goddard and his companions had the final adventure of their kayak voyage.

Two days after they left Cairo—and an enthusiastic welcome there—a crowd of Delta villagers attacked them: foreigners . . . with cameras . . . spies! A police escort with red tarbooshes, rifles, and fine Arabian stallions guarded their final miles.

Would I be taken for a spy? Quite likely,

crop in the country. A Delta farmer and his sons (above) ride a wooden beam to harrow a plot, breaking up clods left by their plow.

Harvest hand, a fellah cuts wheat with a sickle, traditional tool of his ancestors. Egypt manufactures mechanical farm equipment, but many farmers fear that machines will displace them and sow widespread rural unemployment.

my Egyptian friends told me, since few people roam around the beaches—and the coastal defenses—of the country. They advised me to detour from Rashîd and stop in Alexandria to get an escort of my own.

"Very wise," agreed Mounir Ismail, chief of the government press and information office in the city's center. "And I'd love to go myself." In a huge and aging taxi, we zipped back along the coast, my host recalling other Geographic staffmen he had helped in past years.

Goddard and his friends hauled their scarred kayaks from the Nile at Rashîd, so close to the Mediterranean that the river tastes salty here in low-water season. Their amazing adventure in steamy tropics, crawling swamplands, and more than 2,000 miles of deathly desert had taken nine months, and a million paddle strokes.

Mr. Mounir led me down a quay jammed with fishing boats. We stopped at a motor launch named *Abu Shahīn,* a 60-foot, sand-colored craft with elegant lines and iron lacework trimming the bows. Her skipper came ashore to bargain. He looked down at his full pantaloons, scarlet sash, and vest with dozens of pearly buttons, stroked his white beard, smiled, and accepted the six pound-notes I offered. Why did the esteemed foreigner want to go to sea for just an afternoon? But it did not really matter. He welcomed the chance to make use of an idle day.

We chugged in midstream down the wide river until we sighted the Nile's final major

TOR EIGELAND, BLACK STAR

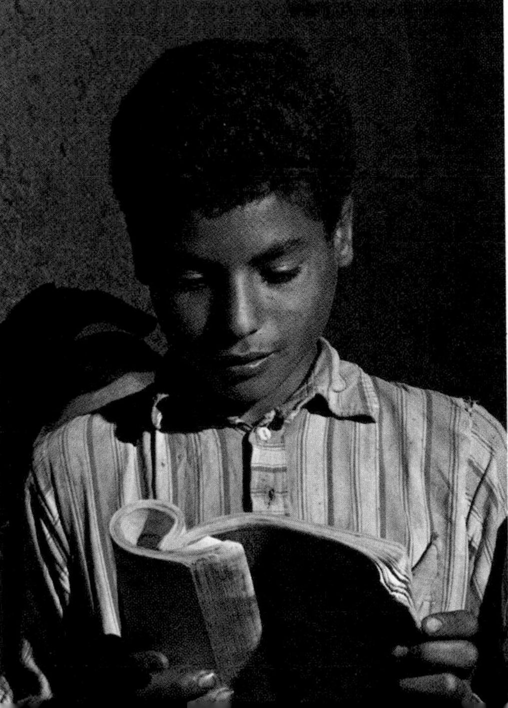

Houses with hats of hay solve space problems in a Nile Delta village. Throughout the region, farmers use rooftops for storage of fodder and fuel to conserve precious land for crops, though the practice creates severe fire hazards. Women in black *malaayas* carry water jars on doughnuts of cloth that ease the burden.

Platter of dough appears to hover between the hands of an Egyptian housewife. Tossing the disk into the air helps make it wafer thin. Baking produces a crisp, tasty bread.

Eager pupil, this Delta boy represents many who left fields to take up textbooks. Increasing emphasis on education in Egypt gets keen response from children. In areas where homes have no electricity, boys often cluster under streetlamps after dark to study schoolwork.

landmark. "Fort St. Julien," the skipper pointed, steering close. The drab crumbled walls seemed hardly worth a glance. But here, in 1799, an officer of Napoleon's local garrison found the stone now known throughout the world by Rashîd's foreign name, Rosetta.

The slab of black basalt records a decree passed by the general council of Egyptian priests when they met at Memphis in 196 B.C. The document says little of importance. Most of it praises the piety and patriotism of Ptolemy V and says the ruler will receive new honors. But the markings that spell it out are extremely important. Chiseled in hieroglyphs, repeated in Egyptian demotic script, then repeated again in Greek, the decree became a key for translating the written language of ancient Egypt. Starting with this stone, scholars unlocked 3,000 years of forgotten civilization.

The sun-baked afternoon felt distinctly cooler now, and gulls overhead sagged like wet newspapers in a strengthening wind. A colonnade of palms along the banks gave way to grasses, then to sand.

Soon nothing barred us from a fiercely pounding sea but the last stringy points of Africa. A single horse carriage glided along the sandspit to the west, and someone waved from a little military post near the end of land. Past the lonely outpost, our boat pitched into charging waves.

"There is a tempest out there," Mr. Mounir translated for the captain. The old man behind the wheel apologized and shook his head. A few hundred yards from our goal we turned back.

But I was not disappointed. I had seen the Nile's end many months before, and then, surely, from the finest point of vantage. A jet soared away from Cairo, climbing fast. The Delta's web of waterways, tan with summer silt, slipped away beneath us. A powerful current flooded past Rashîd. Then water the color of lions rushed beyond the continent, far into the metallic blue of the Mediterranean.

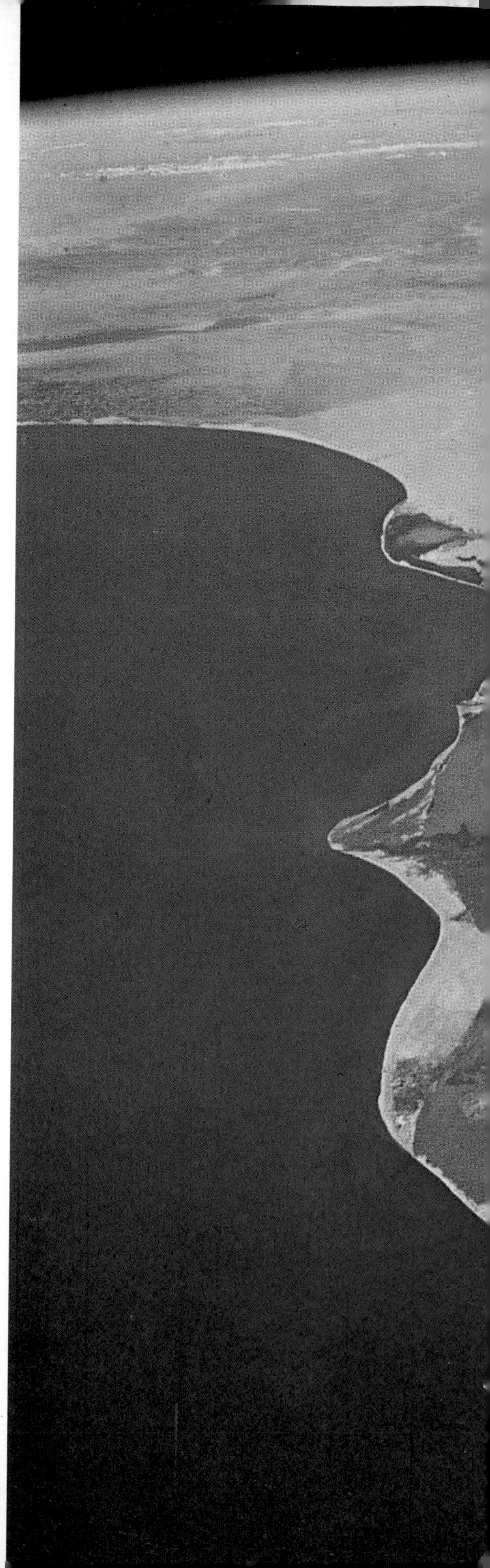

Fertile Nile Delta fans out from Cairo northward, 115 miles below Gemini 4 spacecraft manned by Astronauts James A. McDivitt and Edward H. White. The Suez Canal meets the Mediterranean at the Delta's eastern corner. The Nile's Damietta branch appears vaguely near the Delta's center, and the Rosetta branch, more distinct, wiggles farther west. Suburban Alexandria appears on the coast at bottom.

NASA

INDEX

Illustrations references appear in *italics*. Arabic names with the definite article, *al* or *el*, appear under A or E.

In addition to the maps on pages 24 and 56, this book includes the Society's Atlas Map **Nile Valley—Land of the Pharaohs,** reprinted for this Special Publication. The map, found in the pocket on the inside back cover, has its own index as well as historical notes.

Composition by National Geographic's Phototypographic Division,
Herman J. A. C. Arens, Director; Robert C. Ellis, Jr., Manager
Printed and bound by Fawcett-Haynes Printing Corporation, Rockville, Md.
Color separations by Lanman Engraving Company, Alexandria, Va.; Beck Engraving Compa
Philadelphia, Pa.; and Graphic Color Plate, Inc., Stamford, Conn.